Web Design 10 ..
HTML and CSS for Everyone

30 Lessons to Master the Fundamentals of Responsive and Accessible Web Design

By Alex Tolmachev ©

https://www.linkedin.com/in/alex-tolmachev

Welcome to the HTML and CSS Course!

In this comprehensive course, you will embark on a journey to learn the foundational skills necessary for web development. HTML (HyperText Markup Language) and CSS (Cascading Style Sheets) are the building blocks of the web, allowing you to create structured and visually appealing websites.

What You Will Learn:

1. **HTML Basics**: Understand the structure of HTML documents, including elements, tags, and attributes. You'll learn how to create headings, paragraphs, lists, links, images, and forms.

2. **CSS Fundamentals**: Discover how to style your web pages using CSS. You'll learn about selectors, properties, and how to apply styles to different elements to enhance their appearance.

3. **Responsive Design**: Explore techniques for making your web pages responsive. You'll learn how to use media queries, Flexbox, and CSS Grid to ensure your websites look great on all devices, from desktops to smartphones.

4. **Advanced Features**: Dive into more advanced topics such as CSS transitions and animations, using SVG images, and integrating icon fonts for enhanced visual elements.

5. **Accessibility Best Practices**: Learn the importance of accessibility in web design and how to implement best practices to ensure your websites are usable for everyone, including those with disabilities.

6. **Practical Exercises**: Each lesson will include practical exercises to reinforce your learning. You'll create projects that allow you to apply what you've learned in a hands-on manner.

7. **Capstone Project**: By the end of the course, you'll have the opportunity to create a complete web page project that showcases

your skills, from HTML structure to responsive design and accessibility features.

Who This Course Is For:

- **Beginners**: No prior experience is necessary! This course is designed for anyone interested in learning how to build websites.

- **Aspiring Web Developers**: If you're looking to start a career in web development, this course provides the essential skills needed to get started.

- **Designers**: If you're a graphic designer wanting to understand web technologies better, this course will equip you with the knowledge to collaborate more effectively with developers.

How to Get the Most Out of This Course:

- **Practice Regularly**: Hands-on practice is essential to mastering HTML and CSS. Complete the exercises and projects provided.

- **Experiment**: Don't hesitate to experiment with your own designs and ideas. Creativity is a key aspect of web development.

- **Ask Questions**: If you encounter challenges or have questions, seek help from communities, forums, or your peers.

Conclusion

By the end of this course, you will have a solid understanding of HTML and CSS, enabling you to create beautiful, functional web pages. Join us as we dive into the exciting world of web development and start building your very own websites!

Let's get started!

Course Outline

HTML Fundamentals

CSS Fundamentals

Lesson 1: Introduction to HTML and Web Structure

HTML (HyperText Markup Language) is the backbone of web content. Let's start by creating a basic HTML document. Here's your first task:

1. Open a text editor (like Notepad, VS Code, or Sublime Text).

2. Copy the code below to create a basic HTML structure.

HTML Template

```
<!DOCTYPE html>

<html lang="en">

<head>

  <meta charset="UTF-8">

  <meta name="viewport" content="width=device-width, initial-scale=1.0">

  <title>My First HTML Page</title>

</head>

<body>

  <h1>Welcome to HTML!</h1>

  <p>This is my first paragraph.</p>

</body>

</html>
```

Explanation of the Code:

- **<!DOCTYPE html>**: Declares this document as an HTML5 document.

- **<html lang="en">**: Begins the HTML document and sets the language to English.

- **<head>**: Contains metadata, including the **<title>** tag, which sets the page title in the browser tab.

- **<body>**: Where the content you see on the page goes (like headings, paragraphs, images, and links).

Try creating this file, saving it as **index.html**, and opening it in a browser to see the result.

Lesson 1 Exercises: Introduction to HTML Structure

In this first lesson, your exercises focus on building a basic HTML structure.

Exercise 1: Creating a Simple HTML Document

1. **Objective**: Create a basic HTML document with a title and a heading.

2. **Steps**:

   - Open a text editor (e.g., VS Code).

   - Create a new file and save it as **index.html**.

   - Write the following structure:

     - A **<!DOCTYPE html>** declaration.

     - An **<html>** tag with **<head>** and **<body>** sections.

     - Inside the **<head>**, add a **<title>** with the text "My First Web Page".

     - Inside the **<body>**, add an **<h1>** tag with the text "Hello, World!".

3. **Expected Output**: When opened in a browser, the page title should say "My First Web Page" with an **<h1>** heading displaying "Hello, World!" on the page.

Exercise 2: Adding More Structure

1. **Objective**: Add additional elements to the HTML document.

2. **Steps**:

   - In your index.html file, add a **<p>** paragraph under the **<h1>** with a brief introduction about yourself.

- o Add an **\<h2\>** subheading that says "About Me".

- o Below the **\<h2\>**, add another **\<p\>** paragraph describing your interests or hobbies.

3. **Expected Output**: When opened in a browser, you should see:

- o An **\<h1\>** heading, a **\<p\>** paragraph with a brief intro, an **\<h2\>** heading, and another **\<p\>** describing your hobbies.

Exercise 3: Creating Multiple Sections

1. **Objective**: Organize content with sections.

2. **Steps**:

- o In **index.html**, create a **\<header\>** section containing an **\<h1\>** with your name.

- o Add a **\<main\>** section, where you place your "About Me" section from Exercise 2.

- o Add a **\<footer\>** section with a **\<p\>** saying "Thank you for visiting!".

3. **Expected Output**: The page should have a **\<header\>** with your name, a **\<main\>** section with your "About Me" content, and a \<footer\> at the bottom with a thank-you message.

Lesson 2: Basic HTML Elements – Paragraphs, Headings, and Divisions

In this lesson, we'll explore a few core HTML elements that help structure the content on your page. These are essential for creating a readable layout.

Core Elements

1. **Headings** (<h1> to <h6>): HTML provides six levels of headings, with <h1> being the largest and <h6> the smallest. These are commonly used for titles and section headers.

Example:

<h1>This is an H1 Heading</h1>

<h2>This is an H2 Heading</h2>

<h3>This is an H3 Heading</h3>

2. **Paragraphs** (<p>): The <p> element is used to define paragraphs of text. It's one of the most frequently used tags for body text.

Example:

<p>This is a paragraph of text. You can add more paragraphs to create separate blocks of text.</p>

3. **Divisions** (<div>): The <div> element is a container that groups other elements together. While it doesn't add visual structure on its own, it's helpful for organizing sections and can be styled with CSS later.

Example:

<div>

  <h2>Section Title</h2>

  <p>This paragraph is inside a div.</p>

</div>

Practice Task

1. Create a new HTML file or add to the **index.html** file from Lesson 1.

2. Use the code below as an example to add headings, paragraphs, and divs.

Example HTML Structure

```
<!DOCTYPE html>

<html lang="en">

<head>

  <meta charset="UTF-8">

  <meta name="viewport" content="width=device-width, initial-scale=1.0">

  <title>Basic HTML Elements</title>

</head>

<body>

  <h1>Welcome to My Web Page</h1>

  <h2>About This Page</h2>

  <p>This is a basic example page where we are learning HTML structure.</p>


  <div>

    <h3>Section 1</h3>

    <p>This paragraph is inside a div, which helps organize content.</p>

  </div>
```

```
<div>

    <h3>Section 2</h3>

    <p>Divs are also useful when styling with CSS to control layout and
appearance.</p>

    </div>

</body>

</html>
```

3. Save the file and open it in a browser to see how it looks.

This layout introduces a few more structural elements, setting us up for the next lesson, where we'll cover links and images.

Lesson 2 Exercises: Text Formatting and Headings

In this lesson, you'll practice using various HTML text formatting tags and explore different heading levels.

Exercise 1: Experimenting with Headings

1. **Objective**: Create and style different heading levels to understand the hierarchy.

2. **Steps**:

   o In your **index.html** file, add the following heading levels under your <main> section:

     ▪ <h1> with "Main Heading"

     ▪ <h2> with "Section Heading"

     ▪ <h3> with "Subsection Heading"

     ▪ Continue with <h4>, <h5>, and <h6>, each with a relevant description.

3. **Expected Output**: You should see all six heading levels on your page, each progressively smaller, establishing a visual hierarchy.

Exercise 2: Applying Text Formatting Tags

1. **Objective**: Use various text formatting tags to enhance content.

2. **Steps**:

   o In index.html, create a new paragraph (<p>) under your headings with the following text:

     ▪ "I am **bold** and I am *italic*, and here is a <code> snippet."

o   Use <strong> to bold the word "bold", <em> to italicize "italic", and wrap "code snippet" with <code>.

3. **Expected Output**: The word "bold" should be bolded, "italic" should be italicized, and "code snippet" should appear in a monospace font.

Exercise 3: Adding Quotes and Small Print

1. **Objective**: Use blockquotes, inline quotes, and small text.

2. **Steps**:

   o   Below the paragraph from Exercise 2, add:

      ▪   A <blockquote> with your favorite quote.

      ▪   A sentence that includes an inline quote using <q>.

      ▪   A small print using <small>, such as "This page was last updated in 2023."

3. **Expected Output**: You should see a blockquote for the main quote, an inline quote within a sentence, and small print text.

Lesson 3: Links and Images

Links and images are essential parts of any web page. They allow users to navigate between pages and make the page visually engaging.

Links

Links are created with the <a> (anchor) tag. The **href** attribute specifies the destination URL.

Example of a Link:

<a href="https://www.example.com">Visit Example.com</a>

- **href**: The URL where the link will take the user.

- **Text between <a> and </a>**: This is the clickable text.

You can also create links that open in a new tab by adding the target="_blank" attribute:

<a href="https://www.example.com" target="_blank">Visit Example.com in a new tab</a>

Images

Images are added with the <img> tag, which is self-closing. The src attribute specifies the image URL or file path, and alt provides alternative text (important for accessibility).

Example of an Image:

<img src="https://www.example.com/image.jpg" alt="Description of the image">

- **src**: The source URL of the image.

- **alt**: Describes the image. This text shows if the image doesn't load and is read aloud by screen readers.

Combining Links and Images

You can wrap an image in a link so that clicking the image navigates to a page.

Example:

```
<a href="https://www.example.com">

  <img src="https://www.example.com/image.jpg" alt="Description of the image">

</a>
```

Practice Task

1. Add this code to your HTML file to practice links and images:

```
<!DOCTYPE html>

<html lang="en">

<head>

  <meta charset="UTF-8">

  <meta name="viewport" content="width=device-width, initial-scale=1.0">

  <title>Links and Images</title>

</head>

<body>

  <h1>Links and Images Example</h1>


  <!-- Simple Link -->

  <p><a href="https://www.wikipedia.org">Go to Wikipedia</a></p>


  <!-- Link that Opens in a New Tab -->
```

```
<p><a href="https://www.wikipedia.org" target="_blank">Visit Wikipedia
in a new tab</a></p>


<!-- Image Example -->

<h2>Sample Image</h2>

<img src="https://via.placeholder.com/150" alt="Placeholder image">


<!-- Image Wrapped in a Link -->

<p><a href="https://www.wikipedia.org">

   <img src="https://via.placeholder.com/150" alt="Clickable placeholder
image">

   </a></p>

</body>

</html>
```

2. Save the file and open it in a browser to test the links and view the images.

Try clicking on each link, and observe how the image behaves when wrapped in a link.

Lesson 3 Exercises: Working with Links and Images

In this lesson, you'll practice adding links and images to your HTML page.

Exercise 1: Adding Internal and External Links

1. **Objective**: Create internal and external links within your HTML document.

2. **Steps**:

   - Add a new section to your index.html file with an <h2> heading, titled "Useful Links".

   - Under this heading, add:

     - An external link to a website you like (e.g., "Visit Google") using the <a> tag.

     - An internal link that scrolls to the "About Me" section you created earlier. Use an id on your "About Me" section (e.g., id="about") and link to it with href="#about".

3. **Expected Output**: The page should have a "Useful Links" section with a clickable link to an external website and an internal link that scrolls down to your "About Me" section.

Exercise 2: Adding an Image with Alt Text

1. **Objective**: Add an image to your page and provide meaningful alt text.

2. **Steps**:

   - Add a new <section> under <main> with an <h2> heading titled "Gallery".

      o   Inside this section, add an image of your choice using the <img> tag. Use src to specify the image path (e.g., "my-photo.jpg") and alt to describe the image (e.g., "A beautiful sunset over the ocean").

3. **Expected Output**: You should see an image in the "Gallery" section with alternative text describing the image.

Exercise 3: Opening Links in a New Tab

1. **Objective**: Set a link to open in a new tab.

2. **Steps**:

      o   In the "Useful Links" section, add another external link (e.g., "Visit Wikipedia") with target="_blank" to open it in a new tab.

3. **Expected Output**: Clicking this link should open Wikipedia (or your chosen site) in a new browser tab.

Lesson 4: Lists in HTML – Ordered, Unordered, and Nested Lists

Lists are used to present information in an organized way. HTML supports several types of lists: **unordered lists**, **ordered lists**, and **nested lists**.

1. Unordered Lists

Unordered lists display items with bullet points. They're created with the <ul> tag, and each item inside the list is wrapped in <li> (list item) tags.

Example of an Unordered List:

<ul>

   <li>Item One</li>

```
    <li>Item Two</li>

    <li>Item Three</li>

</ul>
```

2. Ordered Lists

Ordered lists display items with numbers. They're created with the <ol> tag, and each item is wrapped in <li> tags.

Example of an Ordered List:

```
<ol>

  <li>First Item</li>

  <li>Second Item</li>

  <li>Third Item</li>

</ol>
```

3. Nested Lists

You can nest lists inside each other by placing one <ul> or <ol> inside an <li>. This can be useful for showing hierarchical information.

Example of a Nested List:

```
<ul>

  <li>Main Item 1

    <ul>

      <li>Sub Item 1.1</li>

      <li>Sub Item 1.2</li>

    </ul>

  </li>
```

```
      <li>Main Item 2</li>

    </ul>
```

Practice Task

1. Add the code below to your HTML file or create a new one to practice lists.

   Example HTML with Lists

   ```
   <!DOCTYPE html>

   <html lang="en">

   <head>

     <meta charset="UTF-8">

     <meta name="viewport" content="width=device-width, initial-scale=1.0">

     <title>HTML Lists</title>

   </head>

   <body>

     <h1>HTML Lists</h1>


     <!-- Unordered List -->

     <h2>Unordered List</h2>

     <ul>

       <li>Apple</li>

       <li>Banana</li>

       <li>Cherry</li>

     </ul>
   ```

```html
<!-- Ordered List -->
<h2>Ordered List</h2>
<ol>
  <li>Step 1</li>
  <li>Step 2</li>
  <li>Step 3</li>
</ol>

<!-- Nested List -->
<h2>Nested List</h2>
<ul>
  <li>Fruits
    <ul>
      <li>Apple</li>
      <li>Banana</li>
    </ul>
  </li>
  <li>Vegetables
    <ul>
      <li>Carrot</li>
      <li>Broccoli</li>
    </ul>
  </li>
</ul>
</body>
```

```
</html>
```

2. Save the file and open it in your browser to see how the lists appear.

    Observe how the items are arranged in each list type, and experiment by adding more items or nesting deeper.

Lesson 4 Exercises: Working with HTML Lists

In this lesson, you'll practice creating and styling ordered, unordered, and nested lists.

Exercise 1: Creating an Unordered List

1. **Objective**: Create an unordered list of items.

2. **Steps**:

   o Add a new section to your index.html file with an <h2> heading titled "My Hobbies".

   o Below the heading, add an unordered list (<ul>) with at least five hobbies or activities you enjoy (e.g., "Reading", "Traveling", "Cooking").

3. **Expected Output**: You should see a bulleted list of your hobbies.

Exercise 2: Creating an Ordered List

1. **Objective**: Create an ordered list of steps.

2. **Steps**:

   o Add a new section with an <h2> heading titled "My Morning Routine".

   o Below the heading, create an ordered list (<ol>) with at least five steps in your morning routine (e.g., "Wake up", "Brush teeth", "Make coffee").

3. **Expected Output**: You should see a numbered list describing your morning routine.

Exercise 3: Creating a Nested List

1. **Objective**: Create a nested list to show subcategories.

2. **Steps**:

   o   Add a new section with an <h2> heading titled "Favorite Foods".

   o   Inside this section, create an unordered list of food categories (e.g., "Breakfast", "Lunch", "Dinner").

   o   For each category, nest an unordered list with two or three examples of specific foods you enjoy (e.g., under "Breakfast" you might have "Pancakes", "Omelette", "Smoothie").

3. **Expected Output**: You should see an unordered list with food categories, each containing a nested list of specific items.

Lesson 5: HTML Forms – Text Inputs, Buttons, and Labels

Forms are essential for collecting user input on a website. In this lesson, we'll cover basic form elements, including text inputs, buttons, and labels.

1. Basic Form Structure

Forms in HTML are created with the <form> element. The action attribute defines where the form data is sent, and method specifies how the data is sent (usually GET or POST).

Example of a Basic Form:

<form action="/submit-form" method="POST">

  <!-- Form elements go here -->

</form>

2. Text Input Fields

Text inputs allow users to enter single lines of text. They are created with the <input> tag, setting the type attribute to text.

Example of a Text Input:

<input type="text" name="username" placeholder="Enter your name">

- **type="text"**: Specifies that this is a text input.
- **name**: Identifies the data when submitted.
- **placeholder**: Text shown inside the input before the user types.

3. Labels

Labels are added to make form elements more accessible. The <label> element is used, and it can be linked to an input by using the for attribute (matching the id of the input).

Example of a Label with Text Input:

<label for="username">Username:</label>

<input type="text" id="username" name="username" placeholder="Enter your name">

4. Submit Button

The submit button allows users to submit the form. It's created with the <input> tag with type="submit" or the <button> tag with type="submit".

Example of a Submit Button:

<input type="submit" value="Submit">

Or, using a button tag:

<button type="submit">Submit</button>

Practice Task

1. Add the following form code to your HTML file to practice creating a basic form with text inputs, labels, and a submit button.

Example HTML with Form Elements

<!DOCTYPE html>

<html lang="en">

<head>

  <meta charset="UTF-8">

```html
    <meta name="viewport" content="width=device-width, initial-
scale=1.0">
    <title>HTML Forms</title>
</head>
<body>
  <h1>HTML Form Example</h1>


  <!-- Form Structure -->
  <form action="/submit-form" method="POST">

    <!-- Text Input with Label -->
    <label for="username">Username:</label>
    <input type="text" id="username" name="username"
placeholder="Enter your username">


    <br><br>


    <!-- Email Input with Label -->
    <label for="email">Email:</label>
    <input type="email" id="email" name="email" placeholder="Enter your
email">


    <br><br>


    <!-- Submit Button -->
    <button type="submit">Submit</button>
  </form>
```

```
</body>

</html>
```

2. Save the file and open it in your browser. You'll see a form with fields for username and email, along with a submit button.

Experiment by adding more input fields if you'd like.

Lesson 5 Exercises: Building a Basic HTML Form

In this lesson, you'll practice creating a basic form with text inputs, labels, and a submit button.

Exercise 1: Creating a Simple Form with Labels and Text Inputs

1. **Objective**: Create a basic form to collect user information.

2. **Steps**:

   - In your **index.html** file, add a new section with an <h2> heading titled "Contact Us".

   - Create a form with the following fields:

     - A text input for "Name" with an appropriate <label>.

     - An email input for "Email" with an appropriate <label>.

     - A text area for "Message" with an appropriate <label>.

3. **Expected Output**: You should see a form with fields for name, email, and a message, each labeled correctly.

Exercise 2: Adding a Submit Button

1. **Objective**: Add a submit button to the form.

2. **Steps**:

   - Below the "Message" text area in the form, add a submit button (<button type="submit">Send Message</button>).

3. **Expected Output**: The form should have a "Send Message" button, which will attempt to submit the form when clicked.

Exercise 3: Using the placeholder Attribute

1. **Objective**: Use placeholders to guide the user on what to enter.

2. **Steps**:

   o Add placeholder text to the "Name", "Email", and "Message" fields.

      ▪ For example, "Enter your name" in the name field, "Enter your email" in the email field, and "Write your message" in the message text area.

3. **Expected Output**: Each input field should display placeholder text, helping users understand what information to enter.

Lesson 6: More Form Elements – Checkboxes, Radio Buttons, and Select Menus

In this lesson, we'll expand on forms by learning about checkboxes, radio buttons, and select menus. These elements allow users to make selections and choose options.

1. Checkboxes

Checkboxes allow users to select multiple options. Each checkbox is created with an <input> tag, setting type="checkbox".

Example of Checkboxes:

<label>

  <input type="checkbox" name="hobby" value="reading"> Reading

</label>

<label>

  <input type="checkbox" name="hobby" value="sports"> Sports

</label>

<label>

  <input type="checkbox" name="hobby" value="music"> Music

</label>

- **type="checkbox"**: Specifies this input as a checkbox.
- **name**: Groups the checkboxes under the same name for form submission.
- **value**: The value submitted if the checkbox is selected.

2. Radio Buttons

Radio buttons allow users to select only one option within a group. Each radio button is created with an <input> tag, setting type="radio". To group radio buttons, they need the same name.

Example of Radio Buttons:

<label>

  <input type="radio" name="gender" value="male"> Male

</label>

<label>

  <input type="radio" name="gender" value="female"> Female

</label>

<label>

  <input type="radio" name="gender" value="other"> Other

</label>

- **type="radio"**: Specifies this input as a radio button.
- **name**: Groups radio buttons to ensure only one can be selected.
- **value**: The value submitted if this option is selected.

3. Select Menus

The <select> element creates a dropdown menu, with each option inside an <option> tag. Only one option is selectable unless you add the multiple attribute.

Example of a Select Menu:

<label for="country">Country:</label>

<select name="country" id="country">

```
<option value="us">United States</option>

<option value="ca">Canada</option>

<option value="uk">United Kingdom</option>

</select>
```

- **<select>**: The dropdown menu element.
- **<option>**: Each selectable option in the menu.
- **value**: The value submitted when this option is selected.

Practice Task

1. Add this code to your HTML file to practice checkboxes, radio buttons, and a select menu.

Example HTML with Additional Form Elements

```
<!DOCTYPE html>

<html lang="en">

<head>

  <meta charset="UTF-8">

  <meta name="viewport" content="width=device-width, initial-scale=1.0">

  <title>More Form Elements</title>

</head>

<body>

  <h1>Form with Additional Elements</h1>


  <!-- Form Structure -->
```

```
<form action="/submit-form" method="POST">

    <!-- Checkboxes -->

    <h2>Select Your Hobbies:</h2>

    <label><input type="checkbox" name="hobby" value="reading">
Reading</label>

    <label><input type="checkbox" name="hobby" value="sports">
Sports</label>

    <label><input type="checkbox" name="hobby" value="music">
Music</label>


    <br><br>


    <!-- Radio Buttons -->

    <h2>Choose Your Gender:</h2>

    <label><input type="radio" name="gender" value="male"> Male</label>

    <label><input type="radio" name="gender" value="female">
Female</label>

    <label><input type="radio" name="gender" value="other">
Other</label>


    <br><br>


    <!-- Select Menu -->

    <h2>Select Your Country:</h2>

    <label for="country">Country:</label>

    <select name="country" id="country">

      <option value="us">United States</option>
```

```
      <option value="ca">Canada</option>

      <option value="uk">United Kingdom</option>

   </select>


   <br><br>


   <!-- Submit Button -->

   <button type="submit">Submit</button>

  </form>

</body>

</html>
```

2. Save the file and open it in your browser. You'll see a form with checkboxes for hobbies, radio buttons for gender, and a select menu for countries.

Try selecting different options and test how they work.

Lesson 6 Exercises: Using Checkboxes, Radio Buttons, and Select Menus

In this lesson, you'll practice adding form elements that allow users to make selections, such as checkboxes, radio buttons, and dropdown menus.

Exercise 1: Adding Checkboxes

1. **Objective**: Create a set of checkboxes for multiple selections.

2. **Steps**:

   - In the "Contact Us" form you created in Lesson 5, add a section for "Preferred Contact Methods".

   - Under this section, create three checkboxes with the following options: "Email", "Phone", and "Text".

   - Use a <label> for each checkbox to describe the option.

3. **Expected Output**: You should see three checkboxes labeled "Email", "Phone", and "Text", allowing users to select multiple contact methods.

Exercise 2: Adding Radio Buttons

1. **Objective**: Use radio buttons to allow a single selection for gender.

2. **Steps**:

   - Add a new section in the form titled "Gender".

   - Create a group of radio buttons with options for "Male", "Female", and "Other".

   - Use the same name attribute for all radio buttons in this group to ensure only one option can be selected at a time.

   - Add <label> elements for each radio button.

3. **Expected Output**: You should see a group of radio buttons for gender with the options "Male", "Female", and "Other".

Exercise 3: Adding a Select Menu

1. **Objective**: Use a dropdown menu to allow users to select their country.

2. **Steps**:

   o Add a new section titled "Country" in the form.

   o Create a <select> dropdown menu with three or more options representing different countries (e.g., "United States", "Canada", "United Kingdom").

   o Each <option> inside the <select> should have a value and display the country name.

3. **Expected Output**: You should see a dropdown menu with a list of countries.

Lesson 7: HTML Tables

Tables allow us to display data in a structured format with rows and columns. They're created with the <table> element, and we use other elements to define rows, headers, and cells.

Basic Table Structure

1. **<table>**: The main table element.

2. **<tr>**: Defines a row in the table.

3. **<th>**: Defines a header cell, usually bold and centered by default.

4. **<td>**: Defines a standard cell in the table.

Example of a Simple Table:

```
<table>
  <tr>
    <th>Name</th>
    <th>Age</th>
    <th>City</th>
  </tr>
  <tr>
    <td>John</td>
    <td>25</td>
    <td>New York</td>
  </tr>
  <tr>
    <td>Jane</td>
```

```
    <td>30</td>

    <td>Los Angeles</td>

  </tr>

</table>
```

Adding Table Borders

Tables don't have borders by default. You can add borders to make it easier to see the cells.

```
<table border="1">

  <!-- table content -->

</table>
```

Or, you can add CSS later to control the borders.

Table Headers and Footers

For larger tables, <thead>, <tbody>, and <tfoot> can organize content:

- **<thead>**: Contains header rows.

- **<tbody>**: Contains the main data rows.

- **<tfoot>**: Contains footer rows, often used for totals or summary data.

Example of a Table with thead, tbody, and tfoot:

```
<table border="1">

  <thead>

    <tr>

      <th>Product</th>

      <th>Price</th>
```

```
        </tr>
      </thead>
      <tbody>
        <tr>
          <td>Apple</td>
          <td>$1.00</td>
        </tr>
        <tr>
          <td>Banana</td>
          <td>$0.50</td>
        </tr>
      </tbody>
      <tfoot>
        <tr>
          <td>Total</td>
          <td>$1.50</td>
        </tr>
      </tfoot>
    </table>
```

Practice Task

1. Add the following code to your HTML file to practice creating tables with rows, headers, and cells.

Example HTML with Table

```html
<!DOCTYPE html>
<html lang="en">
<head>
  <meta charset="UTF-8">
  <meta name="viewport" content="width=device-width, initial-scale=1.0">
  <title>HTML Tables</title>
</head>
<body>
  <h1>Sample Table</h1>

  <!-- Basic Table -->
  <table border="1">
    <tr>
      <th>Name</th>
      <th>Age</th>
      <th>City</th>
    </tr>
    <tr>
      <td>John</td>
      <td>25</td>
      <td>New York</td>
    </tr>
    <tr>
      <td>Jane</td>
```

```
      <td>30</td>
      <td>Los Angeles</td>
    </tr>
    <tr>
      <td>Sam</td>
      <td>22</td>
      <td>Chicago</td>
    </tr>
</table>
```

```
<h2>Table with Header, Body, and Footer</h2>
<table border="1">
  <thead>
    <tr>
      <th>Product</th>
      <th>Price</th>
    </tr>
  </thead>
  <tbody>
    <tr>
      <td>Apple</td>
      <td>$1.00</td>
    </tr>
    <tr>
      <td>Banana</td>
```

```
        <td>$0.50</td>
      </tr>
    </tbody>
    <tfoot>
      <tr>
        <td>Total</td>
        <td>$1.50</td>
      </tr>
    </tfoot>
  </table>
</body>
</html>
```

2. Save and open the file in your browser. Observe how tables organize data, and try experimenting by adding more rows or modifying the content.

Lesson 7 Exercises: Creating and Structuring Tables

In this lesson, you'll practice creating tables with headers, rows, and cells.

Exercise 1: Creating a Basic Table

1. **Objective**: Create a table to display product details.

2. **Steps**:

   o In your index.html file, add a new section with an <h2> heading titled "Product List".

   o Create a table with three columns: "Product Name", "Price", and "Quantity".

   o Add three rows of data, each representing a different product with a name, price, and quantity.

3. **Expected Output**: You should see a table with a header row and three rows of product information.

Exercise 2: Adding Table Borders

1. **Objective**: Add borders to make the table more readable.

2. **Steps**:

   o In the <table> element, add the border="1" attribute to create a border around each cell.

3. **Expected Output**: The table should now display borders around each cell, making the data easier to read.

Exercise 3: Using <thead>, <tbody>, and <tfoot>

1. **Objective**: Structure the table with table head, body, and foot sections.

2. **Steps:**

   o   Wrap the header row in a <thead> tag.

   o   Wrap the product rows in a <tbody> tag.

   o   Add a <tfoot> tag with a row that shows the total number of items in the "Quantity" column (e.g., "Total", blank cell, and "15" as the total quantity).

3. **Expected Output:** The table should be organized with <thead>, <tbody>, and <tfoot> sections, with a row at the bottom displaying the total quantity.

Lesson 8: Semantic HTML – Using <header>, <footer>, <section>, and More

Semantic HTML elements give meaning to the structure of your webpage. These elements don't change how content appears visually but make it easier for search engines and screen readers to understand the layout.

Key Semantic Elements

1. **<header>**: Defines the header of a section or page, typically containing navigational links or the page title.

2. **<footer>**: Defines the footer of a section or page, often containing copyright info, links, or contact details.

3. **<section>**: Defines a section of content, usually with a heading. It can be used to group related content.

4. **<article>**: Represents independent content, like a blog post or news article. It can stand alone if copied to another context.

5. **<aside>**: Represents sidebar content, related but separate from the main content (e.g., ads, related links).

6. **<nav>**: Defines a navigation section, such as links to other pages or sections of the site.

7. **<main>**: Represents the main content of the page, where the primary content is found. There should only be one <main> per page.

Example Using Semantic Elements

Here's how these elements might look in an HTML structure:

```
<!DOCTYPE html>

<html lang="en">

<head>
```

```html
    <meta charset="UTF-8">

    <meta name="viewport" content="width=device-width, initial-scale=1.0">

    <title>Semantic HTML Example</title>

</head>

<body>

  <!-- Header -->

  <header>

    <h1>My Website</h1>

    <nav>

      <a href="#home">Home</a>

      <a href="#about">About</a>

      <a href="#contact">Contact</a>

    </nav>

  </header>


  <!-- Main Content -->

  <main>

    <!-- Section 1 -->

    <section>

      <h2>About Us</h2>

      <p>This section gives information about our website.</p>

    </section>


    <!-- Article 1 -->
```

```
    <article>

      <h2>Latest Blog Post</h2>

      <p>This is a standalone article or blog post content.</p>

    </article>


    <!-- Aside for Related Links -->

    <aside>

      <h3>Related Links</h3>

      <ul>

        <li><a href="#">Related Link 1</a></li>

        <li><a href="#">Related Link 2</a></li>

      </ul>

    </aside>

  </main>


  <!-- Footer -->

  <footer>

    <p>&copy; 2023 My Website. All rights reserved.</p>

  </footer>

</body>

</html>
```

Explanation of Structure

- **<header>** contains the site title and navigation links.

- **\<main\>** holds the primary content, including a \<section\>, \<article\>, and \<aside\>.

- **\<section\>** organizes content under the heading "About Us."

- **\<article\>** represents a standalone blog post.

- **\<aside\>** provides related links, separate from the main flow of content.

- **\<footer\>** includes copyright information.

Practice Task

1. Add the above code to a new HTML file or within your current one.

2. Save and open it in a browser to see the layout of the page with semantic HTML.

Try modifying the content inside each element to create a basic web page structure.

Lesson 8 Exercises: Using Semantic HTML Elements

In this lesson, you'll practice structuring a webpage using semantic elements like <header>, <footer>, <section>, <article>, and <aside>.

Exercise 1: Creating a Page Structure with Semantic Elements

1. **Objective**: Organize a simple webpage using semantic elements.

2. **Steps**:

   - In your index.html, create the following structure:

     - A <header> section with an <h1> for the page title.

     - A <nav> element with links to "Home", "About", and "Contact" sections.

     - A <main> section that will contain the main content.

     - A <footer> section with a copyright notice.

3. **Expected Output**: Your page should have a structured layout with a header, navigation, main content area, and footer.

Exercise 2: Adding Sections and Articles

1. **Objective**: Add meaningful sections to organize content within the <main> area.

2. **Steps**:

   - Inside the <main> section, create two <section> elements:

     - The first <section> titled "About Us" with a <p> paragraph describing the website or yourself.

     - The second <section> titled "Latest Articles" with two <article> elements.

o Each <article> should contain an <h2> for the title and a <p> with a short description or preview of the article.

3. **Expected Output**: The main content should now include "About Us" and "Latest Articles" sections, with each article displaying a title and short description.

Exercise 3: Using <aside> for Additional Information

1. **Objective**: Add an aside to provide supplementary information.

2. **Steps**:

   o Inside the "Latest Articles" section, add an <aside> element after the articles.

   o Inside <aside>, add a short <p> with additional information, like "Related Links" or "Author Bio".

3. **Expected Output**: The "Latest Articles" section should now include an aside with supplementary information, visually separated from the main articles.

Lesson 9: HTML5 Audio and Video Elements

With HTML5, you can easily add audio and video content to your web pages using the <audio> and <video> elements. These elements offer built-in controls, like play and pause buttons, and can be customized to autoplay, loop, or play in different formats.

1. The <audio> Element

The <audio> element allows you to embed audio files. It requires a src attribute for the audio file and can use controls to allow users to play, pause, and control the volume.

Basic Audio Example:

<audio controls>

   <source src="audio-file.mp3" type="audio/mpeg">

   <source src="audio-file.ogg" type="audio/ogg">

   Your browser does not support the audio element.

</audio>

- **controls**: Adds play, pause, and volume control buttons.
- **<source>**: Allows you to provide multiple audio formats to ensure compatibility across different browsers.
- **Fallback Text**: The text "Your browser does not support the audio element" will appear if the browser doesn't support <audio>.

2. The <video> Element

The <video> element allows you to embed videos in your page. Similar to <audio>, it requires a src attribute and can use controls.

Basic Video Example:

```
<video controls width="400">

    <source src="video-file.mp4" type="video/mp4">

    <source src="video-file.ogg" type="video/ogg">

    Your browser does not support the video element.

</video>
```

- **controls**: Adds play, pause, volume, and fullscreen buttons.
- **width**: Sets the width of the video (you can also set height if needed).
- **Fallback Text**: Displays if the browser doesn't support <video>.

Additional Attributes for <audio> and <video>

- **autoplay**: Starts playing automatically when loaded.
- **loop**: Replays the media in a continuous loop.
- **muted**: Starts playback with the sound muted (often required for autoplay).
- **poster** (for <video>): Sets an image to display before the video starts.

Example of Video with Additional Attributes:

```
<video controls autoplay loop muted width="400" poster="thumbnail.jpg">

    <source src="video-file.mp4" type="video/mp4">

    <source src="video-file.ogg" type="video/ogg">

    Your browser does not support the video element.

</video>
```

Practice Task

1. Add the following code to your HTML file to practice embedding audio and video content.

Example HTML with Audio and Video

```
<!DOCTYPE html>

<html lang="en">

<head>

  <meta charset="UTF-8">

  <meta name="viewport" content="width=device-width, initial-scale=1.0">

  <title>Audio and Video</title>

</head>

<body>

  <h1>HTML5 Audio and Video</h1>


  <!-- Audio Example -->

  <h2>Audio Example</h2>

  <audio controls>

    <source src="audio-file.mp3" type="audio/mpeg">

    <source src="audio-file.ogg" type="audio/ogg">

    Your browser does not support the audio element.

  </audio>


  <!-- Video Example -->

  <h2>Video Example</h2>
```

```
<video controls width="400">

  <source src="video-file.mp4" type="video/mp4">

  <source src="video-file.ogg" type="video/ogg">

  Your browser does not support the video element.

</video>

</body>

</html>
```

2. Replace "audio-file.mp3", "audio-file.ogg", "video-file.mp4", and "video-file.ogg" with actual file paths if you have media files, or experiment with any online file URLs you can find.

Save the file and open it in your browser to test the audio and video controls.

Lesson 9 Exercises: Embedding Audio and Video

In this lesson, you'll practice adding audio and video content to your HTML page with built-in controls.

Exercise 1: Embedding an Audio File

1. **Objective**: Add an audio file to your page with controls for playback.

2. **Steps**:

   o   In your index.html file, add a new section with an <h2> heading titled "Audio".

   o   Add an <audio> element with the controls attribute.

   o   Set the src attribute to an audio file path or URL of your choice (e.g., sample-audio.mp3).

   o   Include a fallback message, such as "Your browser does not support the audio element."

3. **Expected Output**: You should see an audio player with playback controls on your page.

Exercise 2: Embedding a Video File

1. **Objective**: Add a video file to your page with playback controls.

2. **Steps**:

   o   Add another section with an <h2> heading titled "Video".

   o   Insert a <video> element with the controls attribute.

   o   Set the src attribute to a video file path or URL of your choice (e.g., sample-video.mp4).

   o   Include a fallback message, such as "Your browser does not support the video element."

3. **Expected Output**: You should see a video player with playback controls on your page.

Exercise 3: Adding Multiple Sources for Compatibility

1. **Objective**: Provide multiple audio and video sources for better browser compatibility.

2. **Steps**:

   o In the <audio> element, replace the src attribute with two <source> tags for different file formats (e.g., MP3 and OGG).

   o Similarly, update the <video> element to use <source> tags for different formats (e.g., MP4 and OGG).

   o Ensure each <source> has a type attribute specifying the file format (e.g., type="audio/mpeg" for MP3).

3. **Expected Output**: Both the audio and video players should have multiple sources, ensuring they play across different browsers.

Lesson 10: Meta Tags and SEO Basics

Meta tags are HTML tags that provide metadata (information about the webpage) to browsers and search engines. These tags go inside the <head> section and play a crucial role in improving your website's SEO (Search Engine Optimization).

1. Common Meta Tags

- **Charset Meta Tag**: Sets the character encoding of your webpage.

```
<meta charset="UTF-8">
```

- **Viewport Meta Tag**: Controls how your website appears on mobile devices, making it responsive.

```
<meta name="viewport" content="width=device-width, initial-scale=1.0">
```

- **Description Meta Tag**: Provides a short description of your webpage, often shown in search engine results. Keep it concise, around 150-160 characters.

```
<meta name="description" content="This is a brief description of my webpage.">
```

- **Keywords Meta Tag**: Lists keywords related to your page content. Note that modern search engines don't rely on this tag as much, but it's still sometimes used.

```
<meta name="keywords" content="HTML, CSS, tutorial, web development">
```

- **Author Meta Tag**: Specifies the author of the page.

```
<meta name="author" content="Your Name">
```

2. Title Tag

The <title> tag is one of the most important SEO elements. It sets the text that appears on the browser tab and as the clickable headline in search engine results.

```
<title>My Webpage Title</title>
```

3. Open Graph Meta Tags

Open Graph (OG) tags are used by social media platforms to display rich previews when your page is shared. For instance, if you share your page on Facebook, OG tags help control what's displayed.

- **Basic Open Graph Tags**:

```
<meta property="og:title" content="My Webpage Title">
```

```
<meta property="og:description" content="A description of my webpage for social media.">
```

```
<meta property="og:image" content="https://example.com/image.jpg">
```

```
<meta property="og:url" content="https://example.com">
```

4. Robots Meta Tag

The robots meta tag tells search engines if they should index the page and follow the links on it. This is typically used for SEO.

- **Example**:

```
<meta name="robots" content="index, follow">
```

Setting content="noindex, nofollow" would instruct search engines not to index the page or follow links.

Practice Task

1. Add the following code to your HTML file inside the <head> section to practice with meta tags.

Example HTML with Meta Tags

```
<!DOCTYPE html>
```

```html
<html lang="en">
<head>
  <meta charset="UTF-8">
  <meta name="viewport" content="width=device-width, initial-scale=1.0">
  <title>Meta Tags and SEO</title>

  <!-- Meta Tags for SEO -->
  <meta name="description" content="Learn about HTML meta tags and SEO basics in this tutorial.">
  <meta name="keywords" content="HTML, SEO, meta tags, web development">
  <meta name="author" content="Your Name">

  <!-- Open Graph Tags for Social Media -->
  <meta property="og:title" content="Meta Tags and SEO">
  <meta property="og:description" content="A tutorial on using meta tags for better SEO and social media sharing.">
  <meta property="og:image" content="https://example.com/preview.jpg">
  <meta property="og:url" content="https://example.com">
</head>
<body>
  <h1>Welcome to the Meta Tags and SEO Lesson</h1>
  <p>This page contains examples of meta tags that help improve SEO and social media previews.</p>
</body>
</html>
```

2. Save the file and test it. While meta tags don't visibly affect the page in the browser, you can check the source code to see them in action.

Try customizing the tags for your own content or website idea.

Lesson 10 Exercises: Using Meta Tags and SEO

In this lesson, you'll practice adding meta tags to improve SEO and usability, such as descriptions, keywords, and viewport settings.

Exercise 1: Adding a Meta Description

1. **Objective**: Add a meta description for search engines to display in search results.

2. **Steps**:

   o In the <head> section of index.html, add a <meta> tag with the name attribute set to "description".

   o Set the content attribute to a brief description of your webpage (e.g., "A personal portfolio showcasing my projects and skills").

3. **Expected Output**: Your HTML page should have a meta description tag in the <head> section, which search engines can display.

Exercise 2: Adding Keywords and Author Meta Tags

1. **Objective**: Use keywords and author meta tags to provide more information about the page.

2. **Steps**:

   o In the <head> section, add two new <meta> tags:

   ▪ One with name="keywords" and content with relevant keywords (e.g., "portfolio, web development, projects").

   ▪ Another with name="author" and your name in the content attribute.

3. **Expected Output**: You should have two additional meta tags: one for keywords and one for the author's name.

Exercise 3: Setting the Viewport for Mobile Responsiveness

1. **Objective**: Add a meta tag to make your site responsive on mobile devices.

2. **Steps**:

   o   In the <head> section, add a <meta> tag with name="viewport" and content="width=device-width, initial-scale=1.0".

3. **Expected Output**: Your page should now be set up for responsiveness, adjusting to fit the width of any screen.

Lesson 11: Introduction to CSS – Inline, Internal, and External Styles

CSS (Cascading Style Sheets) is a language used to style HTML content. It allows you to change colors, fonts, layout, and more. There are three main ways to add CSS to your HTML: **inline CSS**, **internal CSS**, and **external CSS**.

1. Inline CSS

Inline CSS applies styles directly to an HTML element using the style attribute. While convenient, inline CSS can clutter HTML and is best used sparingly.

Example of Inline CSS:

```
<p style="color: blue; font-size: 18px;">This is a styled paragraph.</p>
```

2. Internal CSS

Internal CSS is added within a <style> tag in the <head> section of your HTML document. It's useful for styling a single page.

Example of Internal CSS:

```
<!DOCTYPE html>

<html lang="en">

<head>

  <meta charset="UTF-8">

  <meta name="viewport" content="width=device-width, initial-scale=1.0">

  <title>Internal CSS Example</title>

  <style>

    body {
```

```
        font-family: Arial, sans-serif;

    }

    h1 {
        color: green;

    }

    p {
        color: blue;

        font-size: 18px;

    }

  </style>

</head>

<body>

  <h1>Welcome to My Web Page</h1>

  <p>This is a paragraph with internal CSS styling.</p>

</body>

</html>
```

3. External CSS

External CSS is stored in a separate file with a .css extension, such as **styles.css**. The HTML file links to this CSS file with the <link> tag. External CSS is the preferred method for larger projects, as it keeps HTML and CSS separate.

Example of External CSS File (styles.css):

```
body {

  font-family: Arial, sans-serif;

}
```

```css
h1 {
  color: green;
}


p {
  color: blue;
  font-size: 18px;
}
```

Linking an External CSS File in HTML:

```html
<!DOCTYPE html>
<html lang="en">
<head>
  <meta charset="UTF-8">
  <meta name="viewport" content="width=device-width, initial-scale=1.0">
  <title>External CSS Example</title>
  <link rel="stylesheet" href="styles.css">
</head>
<body>
  <h1>Welcome to My Web Page</h1>
  <p>This is a paragraph styled with external CSS.</p>
</body>
</html>
```

Practice Task

1. Create a new HTML file and a separate CSS file.

2. Add the CSS code to your styles.css file, and link it in your HTML file.

Example HTML and CSS Files

HTML File: index.html

```
<!DOCTYPE html>
<html lang="en">
<head>
  <meta charset="UTF-8">
  <meta name="viewport" content="width=device-width, initial-scale=1.0">
  <title>CSS Basics</title>
  <link rel="stylesheet" href="styles.css">
</head>
<body>
  <h1>Styling with CSS</h1>
  <p>This paragraph is styled using external CSS.</p>
</body>
</html>
```

CSS File: styles.css

```
body {
```

```
    font-family: Arial, sans-serif;

}


h1 {

    color: teal;

    text-align: center;

}


p {

    color: darkblue;

    font-size: 20px;

    line-height: 1.6;

}
```

3. Save both files and open **index.html** in your browser to see the styled content.

This setup will prepare you for more complex styling as we move forward.

Lesson 11 Exercises: Applying CSS with Inline, Internal, and External Styles

In this lesson, you'll practice applying CSS in different ways to style your HTML page.

Exercise 1: Using Inline CSS

1. **Objective**: Apply inline CSS to style a specific HTML element.

2. **Steps**:

   - In your index.html file, add an inline style to an <h1> element in the <body> section.

   - Set the style attribute to change the color (e.g., style="color: blue;").

3. **Expected Output**: The <h1> heading should display in the specified color.

Exercise 2: Using Internal CSS

1. **Objective**: Use internal CSS to style multiple elements.

2. **Steps**:

   - In the <head> section of index.html, add a <style> tag.

   - Inside the <style> tag, add the following styles:

     - Set the background color of the <body> to a light shade (e.g., #f0f0f0).

     - Style all <p> tags to have a font size of 18px.

3. **Expected Output**: Your page's background should change color, and all paragraphs should display with the specified font size.

Exercise 3: Using External CSS

1. **Objective**: Create an external CSS file to style the entire webpage.

2. **Steps**:

   o   In your project folder, create a new file named styles.css.

   o   In styles.css, add styles to:

   - Set the font family for the entire page to Arial, sans-serif.

   - Change the color of all <h2> elements to #3498db.

   o   Link styles.css to your HTML file by adding <link rel="stylesheet" href="styles.css"> in the <head> section.

3. **Expected Output**: Your external CSS file should apply the specified styles to the page, changing the font family and heading color.

Lesson 12: Basic CSS Properties – Color, Font, and Background

Now that you know how to add CSS to your HTML, let's explore some basic CSS properties for styling text, backgrounds, and colors. These properties are essential for enhancing the look and feel of your page.

1. Color

The color property changes the text color of an element. You can specify colors using different formats, such as **color names**, **hex codes**, **RGB**, or **HSL**.

Examples:

```
p {
    color: red; /* Color name */
}
```

```
h1 {
    color: #3498db; /* Hex code */
}
```

```
h2 {
    color: rgb(255, 99, 71); /* RGB */
}
```

```
h3 {
    color: hsl(120, 100%, 50%); /* HSL */
}
```

2. Font Properties

CSS offers several properties to control font styles, such as font-family, font-size, font-weight, and font-style.

- **font-family**: Specifies the font type.

```
body {
   font-family: Arial, sans-serif;
}
```

- **font-size**: Sets the size of the font.

```
h1 {
   font-size: 36px;
}
```

- **font-weight**: Controls the thickness of the text (e.g., bold).

```
h2 {
   font-weight: bold;
}
```

- **font-style**: Sets text as italic.

```
p {
   font-style: italic;
}
```

3. Background

The background property allows you to set a background color, image, or other styles.

- **Background Color**: The background-color property changes the background color of an element.

```
body {

  background-color: #f0f8ff;

}
```

- **Background Image**: The background-image property sets an image as the background.

```
body {

  background-image: url('background.jpg');

}
```

- **Background Position, Size, and Repeat**: Additional properties to control the position, size, and repetition of background images.

```
body {

  background-image: url('background.jpg');

  background-position: center;

  background-size: cover;

  background-repeat: no-repeat;

}
```

Practice Task

1. Update your styles.css file with the following CSS properties to apply colors, fonts, and background styles to different elements.

Example CSS File (styles.css):

```
/* Text Color */

h1 {

  color: #3498db;

}
```

```css
p {
  color: rgb(34, 139, 34);
}

/* Font Styling */
body {
  font-family: Arial, sans-serif;
}

h2 {
  font-size: 24px;
  font-weight: bold;
  font-style: italic;
}

/* Background Styling */
body {
  background-color: #f0f8ff;
}

div {
  background-color: #dcdcdc;
  padding: 20px;
  border-radius: 10px;
```

}

2. If you want to try a background image, add the background-image property in the body selector and use an image URL or path.

3. Save and open **index.html** in your browser to see the updated styles.

This lesson gives you control over basic visual aspects of your page, making it look more polished.

Lesson 12 Exercises: Working with Color, Font, and Background Properties

In this lesson, you'll practice using CSS properties to style text, backgrounds, and fonts.

Exercise 1: Changing Text Color

1. **Objective**: Use the color property to style different elements.

2. **Steps**:

   o In styles.css, set the text color of all <p> elements to #333333.

   o Change the text color of <h1> elements to #2980b9.

3. **Expected Output**: All paragraphs should display in dark gray (#333333), and <h1> headings should display in blue (#2980b9).

Exercise 2: Applying Font Styles

1. **Objective**: Use font properties to enhance text.

2. **Steps**:

   o In styles.css, set the font family for <body> to "Helvetica, Arial, sans-serif".

   o Set the font size of <h2> elements to 28px.

   o Make all <strong> elements bold by adding font-weight: bold;.

3. **Expected Output**: Your page should display in Helvetica or Arial font, and <h2> elements should appear larger, while <strong> elements are bold.

Exercise 3: Adding a Background Color

1. **Objective**: Apply a background color to specific sections.

2. **Steps**:

   o In styles.css, set a light background color (e.g., #f9f9f9) for your main content section (e.g., <main>).

   o Add a different background color (e.g., #e0e0e0) to the <footer>.

3. **Expected Output**: The <main> section should have a light background color, while the <footer> displays with a slightly darker background.

Lesson 13: CSS Selectors and Combinators

CSS selectors are patterns used to select and style specific elements in HTML. Understanding how to target elements precisely is essential for creating clean, efficient styles. We'll also cover **combinators**, which allow you to select elements based on their relationships.

1. Basic Selectors

- **Universal Selector (*)**: Selects all elements.

```
* {
  margin: 0;
  padding: 0;
}
```

- **Type Selector**: Selects all elements of a specific type (e.g., all <p> elements).

```
p {
  color: blue;
}
```

- **Class Selector (.)**: Selects elements with a specific class. Use a period (.) before the class name.

```
.highlight {
  background-color: yellow;
}
```

- **ID Selector (#)**: Selects a unique element with a specific ID. Use a hash (#) before the ID name.

```
#main-header {
  font-size: 24px;
  color: green;
```

}

2. Attribute Selector

Selects elements based on the presence or value of an attribute.

input[type="text"] {

   border: 1px solid gray;

}

3. Pseudo-classes

Pseudo-classes target elements based on their state or position.

- **:hover**: Styles an element when hovered.

a:hover {

   color: red;

}

- **:first-child**: Targets the first child of a parent.

p:first-child {

   font-weight: bold;

}

4. Combinators

Combinators are used to select elements based on relationships with other elements.

- **Descendant Combinator (Space)**: Selects elements nested within a specified parent.

div p {

   color: purple;

```
}
```

- **Child Combinator (>)**: Selects direct children of an element.

```
div > p {
    font-size: 18px;
}
```

- **Adjacent Sibling (+)**: Selects the immediate sibling of an element.

```
h2 + p {
    margin-top: 0;
}
```

- **General Sibling (~)**: Selects all siblings of an element.

```
h2 ~ p {
    color: gray;
}
```

Practice Task

1. Update your styles.css file with the following CSS rules to practice different selectors and combinators.

Example CSS File (styles.css):

```
/* Universal Selector */

* {
    box-sizing: border-box;
}


/* Type Selector */
```

```
h1 {

  color: #3498db;

}


/* Class Selector */

.highlight {

  background-color: yellow;

  padding: 5px;

}


/* ID Selector */

#main-header {

  font-size: 26px;

  color: green;

  text-align: center;

}


/* Attribute Selector */

input[type="text"] {

  border: 1px solid #ccc;

  padding: 5px;

}


/* Pseudo-class */

a:hover {
```

```css
    color: red;
}


/* Descendant Combinator */
div p {
    color: darkblue;
}


/* Child Combinator */
div > p {
    font-style: italic;
}


/* Adjacent Sibling */
h2 + p {
    margin-top: 0;
    color: darkgreen;
}


/* General Sibling */
h2 ~ p {
    color: gray;
}
```

2. Save the file and open index.html in your browser to test each selector.

These selectors give you powerful control over styling specific elements on your page.

Lesson 13 Exercises: Practicing CSS Selectors and Combinators

In this lesson, you'll work with different CSS selectors and combinators to target elements based on relationships and states.

Exercise 1: Using Class and ID Selectors

1. **Objective**: Style elements with class and ID selectors.

2. **Steps**:

   o In index.html, add a class="highlight" to one of your <p> elements and an id="main-header" to your main <h1>.

   o In styles.css, add:

      ▪ A class selector .highlight to change the background color to #f0f8ff.

      ▪ An ID selector #main-header to change the font color to #3498db.

3. **Expected Output**: The paragraph with the highlight class should have a light blue background, and the <h1> with id="main-header" should display in blue.

Exercise 2: Using Descendant and Child Combinators

1. **Objective**: Style nested elements using combinators.

2. **Steps**:

   o In index.html, add a list inside a <div> (e.g., <div><ul>...</ul></div>).

   o In styles.css, add:

      ▪ A descendant selector to target all <li> elements inside a <div> and change their color to #333.

- A child combinator to target only direct child paragraphs (<p>) inside <main> and set their font size to 18px.

3. **Expected Output**: All list items inside the <div> should have a dark gray color, and only direct child paragraphs in <main> should appear with a larger font size.

Exercise 3: Applying Pseudo-classes

1. **Objective**: Use pseudo-classes to style interactive states.

2. **Steps**:

   o In styles.css, add:

   - A :hover effect on links (a:hover) that changes the color to #2980b9.

   - A :first-child selector on <li> items to make the first list item bold.

3. **Expected Output**: Links should change color when hovered, and the first item in any list should be bold.

Lesson 14: The Box Model – Padding, Border, Margin, and Content

The **CSS box model** defines the layout and spacing for every HTML element. Understanding how the box model works will help you control the size, padding, borders, and margins of elements on your page.

1. Components of the Box Model

Each element's box consists of four parts:

1. **Content**: The actual content of the element, like text or an image.

2. **Padding**: Space between the content and the border.

3. **Border**: A line surrounding the padding (if set).

4. **Margin**: Space outside the border, creating distance between this element and others.

Here's a visual representation of how the box model components are layered:

2. Setting Box Model Properties

- **Padding**: Adds space between the content and border. You can set padding for all sides, or each side individually.

```
.box {

    padding: 20px; /* All sides */

    padding-top: 10px;

    padding-right: 15px;

    padding-bottom: 10px;

    padding-left: 15px;

}
```

- **Border**: Adds a border around the content and padding. You can control its width, style, and color.

```
.box {

    border: 2px solid black;

}
```

- **Margin**: Creates space outside the border. Like padding, you can set margins for all sides or each side individually.

```
.box {

    margin: 10px; /* All sides */

    margin-top: 5px;

    margin-right: 15px;

    margin-bottom: 5px;

    margin-left: 15px;

}
```

3. Box Sizing

By default, the width and height of an element include only the content, excluding padding and border. Using box-sizing: border-box ensures padding and borders are included in the width and height, making layout easier to manage.

```css
.box {

  width: 200px;

  height: 100px;

  padding: 20px;

  border: 2px solid black;

  box-sizing: border-box; /* Includes padding and border in width and height */

}
```

Practice Task

1. Update your styles.css file to experiment with box model properties.

Example CSS File (styles.css):

```css
/* Box Model Example */

.container {

  width: 300px;

  background-color: #f0f8ff;

  padding: 20px;

  border: 5px solid #3498db;

  margin: 20px auto; /* Centered horizontally */

  box-sizing: border-box;

}
```

```css
.content-box {

    background-color: #dcdcdc;

    padding: 10px;

    border: 2px dashed #333;

    margin: 15px;

}
```

2. Add the HTML below in your index.html file to test the box model styles.

Example HTML (index.html):

```html
<div class="container">

    <h2>Main Container</h2>

    <p>This container demonstrates padding, border, and margin.</p>


    <div class="content-box">

        <p>Nested box with padding, border, and margin.</p>

    </div>

</div>
```

3. Save both files and open index.html in your browser. Notice how padding, border, and margin affect the spacing and overall size of each element.

The box model is fundamental to layout in CSS, and understanding it will help as we move into positioning and layout techniques.

Lesson 14 Exercises: Working with the CSS Box Model

In this lesson, you'll practice using padding, border, and margin properties to adjust element spacing.

Exercise 1: Adding Padding to Elements

1. **Objective**: Add padding to an element to create space around the content.

2. **Steps**:

   o In styles.css, add padding to your main content area (e.g., <main>).

   o Set padding: 20px; to add space around the content.

3. **Expected Output**: The main content section should have extra space inside, pushing the text away from the edges.

Exercise 2: Adding a Border

1. **Objective**: Apply a border to an element for visual emphasis.

2. **Steps**:

   o In styles.css, add a border to one of your sections (e.g., "About Us" or "Contact").

   o Set a border: 2px solid #333; to apply a solid border around the section.

3. **Expected Output**: The section should have a visible border around it, making it stand out on the page.

Exercise 3: Adjusting Margins for Spacing

1. **Objective**: Use margins to create space between elements.

2. **Steps:**

   o In styles.css, add margin-top: 20px; to your <h2> headings to add space above them.

   o Add margin-bottom: 10px; to <p> elements to add space below each paragraph.

3. **Expected Output**: Headings should have more space above them, and paragraphs should have space below them, improving readability.

Exercise 4: Setting box-sizing to border-box

1. **Objective**: Set box-sizing to include padding and borders in the element's width and height.

2. **Steps:**

   o In styles.css, add box-sizing: border-box; to your <main> section.

   o Observe how the padding and border are included in the section's overall dimensions.

3. **Expected Output**: The main section's width should remain consistent even with padding and borders applied.

Lesson 15: CSS Positioning – Static, Relative, Absolute, and Fixed

CSS positioning allows you to control the placement of elements on a webpage. There are several positioning values, each with different behaviors and applications.

1. Position Property Values

1. **Static (default)**: Elements are positioned according to the normal document flow, with no special positioning applied. This is the default behavior.

```
.static-box {

    position: static;

}
```

2. **Relative**: The element is positioned relative to its normal position. You can adjust its position using the top, right, bottom, and left properties.

```
.relative-box {

    position: relative;

    top: 10px; /* Moves 10px down from its original position */

    left: 20px; /* Moves 20px right from its original position */

}
```

3. **Absolute**: The element is positioned relative to its nearest positioned ancestor (an ancestor with position other than static). If no positioned ancestor is found, it is positioned relative to the <html> element (viewport).

```
.absolute-box {

    position: absolute;
```

```
    top: 50px; /* Moves 50px down from the positioned ancestor or viewport
*/

    left: 30px; /* Moves 30px right */

}
```

4. **Fixed:** The element is positioned relative to the viewport. It stays in the same place even when scrolling.

```
.fixed-box {

    position: fixed;

    top: 0;

    right: 0;

    background-color: yellow;

}
```

5. **Sticky:** The element toggles between relative and fixed, based on the user's scroll position. It behaves like relative until it reaches a specified scroll position, then it "sticks" like fixed.

```
.sticky-box {

    position: sticky;

    top: 20px;

}
```

2. Z-Index

The z-index property controls the stacking order of positioned elements. Higher values appear on top of lower values. z-index only works on positioned elements (those with position other than static).

```
.overlay {

    position: absolute;

    top: 0;
```

```
  left: 0;

  z-index: 10; /* Higher number means it appears above other elements */

}
```

Practice Task

1. Update your styles.css file to practice different position values.

Example CSS File (styles.css):

```css
/* Static (default) */

.static-box {

  width: 150px;

  height: 100px;

  background-color: lightgray;

  border: 1px solid #333;

  margin: 10px;

}


/* Relative */

.relative-box {

  position: relative;

  top: 20px;

  left: 20px;

  background-color: lightblue;

  padding: 10px;

}
```

```css
/* Absolute */
.absolute-box {
    position: absolute;
    top: 50px;
    right: 30px;
    width: 150px;
    background-color: lightgreen;
    padding: 10px;
}

/* Fixed */
.fixed-box {
    position: fixed;
    top: 0;
    left: 0;
    width: 100px;
    height: 50px;
    background-color: yellow;
    text-align: center;
}

/* Sticky */
.sticky-box {
    position: sticky;
```

```
  top: 10px;

  background-color: lightcoral;

  padding: 10px;

  margin: 10px 0;

}
```

2. Add the following HTML code to index.html to test positioning.

Example HTML (index.html):

```
<div class="static-box">Static Box</div>


<div class="relative-box">Relative Box</div>


<div class="absolute-box">Absolute Box (Positioned at top right)</div>


<div class="fixed-box">Fixed Box</div>


<p style="margin-top: 200px;">Scroll down to see the sticky box effect.</p>


<div class="sticky-box">Sticky Box (Sticks when scrolling)</div>


<p>Content goes here. Keep scrolling to test the sticky positioning.</p>
<p>More content here.</p>
```

3. Save both files and open index.html in your browser. Observe how each positioning type behaves.

Experiment by changing values and seeing how elements interact with each other, especially with relative, absolute, and z-index.

Lesson 15 Exercises: Practicing CSS Positioning

In this lesson, you'll experiment with different positioning techniques to control the layout of elements.

Exercise 1: Applying Relative Positioning

1. **Objective**: Use relative positioning to move an element from its normal position.

2. **Steps**:

   o In styles.css, add position: relative; to one of your <h2> elements.

   o Use top: 10px; and left: 20px; to move the heading down and to the right.

3. **Expected Output**: The <h2> element should shift slightly from its original position while maintaining space in the layout.

Exercise 2: Using Absolute Positioning

1. **Objective**: Position an element absolutely within a container.

2. **Steps**:

   o In index.html, wrap a small element (e.g., <div> or <span>) inside a container like <section>.

   o In styles.css, add position: absolute; to the inner element, with top: 10px; and right: 10px;.

   o Set the container's position to relative to make it the reference for the absolute positioning.

3. **Expected Output**: The inner element should be positioned 10px from the top-right corner of its container.

Exercise 3: Creating a Fixed Navigation Bar

1. **Objective**: Use fixed positioning to keep an element visible when scrolling.

2. **Steps**:

   - In index.html, add a <nav> element at the top of your page with links for navigation (e.g., "Home", "About", "Contact").

   - In styles.css, add position: fixed;, top: 0;, and width: 100%; to the <nav>.

   - Add background-color and padding to make it stand out, and add padding-top: 50px; to <body> to prevent content overlap.

3. **Expected Output**: The navigation bar should stay fixed at the top of the page when scrolling.

Exercise 4: Experimenting with Z-Index

1. **Objective**: Use z-index to layer elements.

2. **Steps**:

   - Add two overlapping elements (e.g., <div> elements with background colors).

   - In styles.css, set position: relative; and z-index: 1; for one of the elements, and z-index: 2; for the other.

3. **Expected Output**: The element with the higher z-index should appear above the other in the stacking order.

Lesson 16: Flexbox Layout Basics

CSS Flexbox (Flexible Box) is a layout model that helps distribute space and align items in a container, even when their sizes are unknown or dynamic. Flexbox is especially useful for creating responsive layouts.

1. Setting Up a Flex Container

To use Flexbox, you start by setting display: flex; on a container element. This makes the container a **flex container**, and all direct children become **flex items**.

```
.container {

  display: flex;

}
```

2. Flex Direction

The flex-direction property defines the direction of flex items within the container.

- **Row** (default): Items are arranged horizontally.

```
.container {

  flex-direction: row;

}
```

- **Column**: Items are arranged vertically.

```
.container {

  flex-direction: column;

}
```

3. Justify Content

The justify-content property aligns items along the **main axis** (horizontal by default). It controls the horizontal alignment when flex-direction: row and vertical alignment when flex-direction: column.

- **center**: Centers items.
- **space-between**: Adds space between items.
- **space-around**: Adds space around items.

```
.container {
    justify-content: center; /* Center items horizontally */
}
```

4. Align Items

The align-items property aligns items along the **cross axis** (vertical by default). It controls vertical alignment when flex-direction: row and horizontal alignment when flex-direction: column.

- **center**: Centers items vertically.
- **flex-start**: Aligns items at the start of the cross axis.
- **flex-end**: Aligns items at the end of the cross axis.

```
.container {
    align-items: center; /* Center items vertically */
}
```

5. Flex Wrap

The flex-wrap property controls whether items should wrap onto multiple lines if they don't fit in a single line.

- **nowrap** (default): Items stay on a single line.
- **wrap**: Items wrap onto new lines as needed.

- **wrap-reverse**: Items wrap onto new lines in reverse order.

.container {

  flex-wrap: wrap;

}

6. Flex Item Properties

Each flex item can also be individually controlled with properties like flex-grow, flex-shrink, and flex-basis.

- **flex-grow**: Specifies how much an item should grow relative to others.

.item {

  flex-grow: 1; /* Item takes up remaining space */

}

- **flex-shrink**: Specifies how much an item should shrink relative to others.

.item {

  flex-shrink: 1; /* Item shrinks if necessary */

}

- **flex-basis**: Specifies the initial size of an item before space distribution.

.item {

  flex-basis: 200px; /* Initial size of item */

}

Practice Task

1. Update your styles.css file to apply Flexbox layout properties to a container and items.

Example CSS File (styles.css):

```css
/* Flex Container */
.flex-container {
    display: flex;
    flex-direction: row; /* Arrange items horizontally */
    justify-content: space-around; /* Space between items */
    align-items: center; /* Center items vertically */
    flex-wrap: wrap; /* Allow items to wrap */
    background-color: #f0f8ff;
    padding: 20px;
    border: 2px solid #333;
}


/* Flex Items */
.flex-item {
    background-color: #3498db;
    color: white;
    padding: 20px;
    margin: 10px;
    flex-grow: 1; /* Allow items to grow */
    text-align: center;
}
```

2. Add the following HTML code to index.html to create a Flexbox layout with multiple items.

Example HTML (index.html):

```
<div class="flex-container">

    <div class="flex-item">Item 1</div>

    <div class="flex-item">Item 2</div>

    <div class="flex-item">Item 3</div>

    <div class="flex-item">Item 4</div>

    <div class="flex-item">Item 5</div>

</div>
```

3. Save both files and open index.html in your browser. Notice how the items respond to resizing, wrapping when the container's width changes.

Experiment with different justify-content, align-items, and flex-direction values to see how they affect layout.

Lesson 16 Exercises: Practicing Flexbox Layout

In this lesson, you'll use Flexbox properties to create flexible and responsive layouts.

Exercise 1: Setting Up a Flex Container

1. **Objective**: Make a container a flex container and align items horizontally.

2. **Steps**:

   - In index.html, create a <div class="flex-container"> and add three <div> child elements with sample content (e.g., "Item 1", "Item 2", "Item 3").

   - In styles.css, add display: flex; to .flex-container.

   - Set justify-content: space-around; to space the items evenly across the container.

3. **Expected Output**: The items should be arranged in a horizontal row, with equal space around each item.

Exercise 2: Using Flex Direction

1. **Objective**: Arrange flex items vertically.

2. **Steps**:

   - In styles.css, add flex-direction: column; to .flex-container.

3. **Expected Output**: The items should now stack vertically inside the container.

Exercise 3: Aligning Items in the Center

1. **Objective**: Center align items horizontally and vertically.

2. **Steps**:

   o In styles.css, set justify-content: center; and align-items: center; for .flex-container.

   o Add height: 300px; to .flex-container to create more space.

3. **Expected Output**: All items should be centered within the container, both horizontally and vertically.

Exercise 4: Experimenting with Flex Wrap

1. **Objective**: Allow items to wrap onto multiple lines.

2. **Steps**:

   o Add more items inside .flex-container in index.html until there are at least six items.

   o In styles.css, add flex-wrap: wrap; to .flex-container.

   o Set flex-basis: 45%; for each item to make them wrap within the container.

3. **Expected Output**: The items should wrap onto multiple lines within the container, adjusting to available space.

Exercise 5: Controlling Flex Item Growth

1. **Objective**: Control how flex items grow.

2. **Steps**:

   o In styles.css, set flex-grow: 1; on the first item in .flex-container to allow it to take up more space.

3. **Expected Output**: The first item should expand to take up additional space, while the others remain their original size.

Lesson 17: Responsive Design with Media Queries

Responsive design ensures that your website looks good on devices of all sizes, from mobile phones to desktop monitors. Media queries allow you to apply different styles based on the screen size, orientation, or other device characteristics.

1. Basic Media Query Syntax

A media query starts with @media, followed by a condition. If the condition is met, the enclosed CSS rules are applied.

Example:

```
@media (max-width: 600px) {

  body {

    background-color: lightblue;

  }

}
```

In this example, the background color changes to light blue if the viewport width is 600 pixels or less.

2. Common Media Query Breakpoints

Breakpoints are screen widths where the design changes to better fit the device. Common breakpoints are:

- **Large screens** (desktops): min-width: 992px

- **Tablets**: min-width: 768px and max-width: 991px

- **Mobile phones**: max-width: 767px

3. Applying Different Layouts with Media Queries

Media queries are often used to adjust layout, font sizes, and other styles to improve usability on smaller screens.

Example: Changing Layout with Flexbox and Media Queries

```css
/* Default layout (desktop) */

.flex-container {

    display: flex;

    flex-direction: row;

}


/* Tablet layout */

@media (max-width: 991px) {

    .flex-container {

        flex-direction: column;

        align-items: center;

    }

}


/* Mobile layout */

@media (max-width: 767px) {

    .flex-container {

        flex-direction: column;

        align-items: center;

    }
```

```
.flex-item {

    padding: 15px;

    font-size: 16px;

  }

}
```

4. Hiding Elements on Smaller Screens

Media queries can also hide elements on specific screen sizes, improving the mobile experience by removing unnecessary content.

Example:

```
/* Hide element on mobile */

@media (max-width: 767px) {

  .desktop-only {

    display: none;

  }

}
```

5. Fluid Typography

You can use media queries to adjust font sizes for readability across different screen sizes.

Example:

```
h1 {

  font-size: 32px;

}


@media (max-width: 600px) {
```

```css
h1 {

    font-size: 24px;

  }

}
```

Practice Task

1. Update your styles.css file to include media queries for different screen sizes.

Example CSS File (styles.css):

```css
/* Default Flex Layout for Desktop */

.flex-container {

    display: flex;

    flex-direction: row;

    justify-content: space-between;

    align-items: center;

}


/* Flex Layout for Tablets */

@media (max-width: 991px) {

  .flex-container {

    flex-direction: column;

  }

  .flex-item {

    width: 80%;
```

```css
      margin-bottom: 10px;

   }

}


/* Flex Layout for Mobile */

@media (max-width: 767px) {

  .flex-container {

    flex-direction: column;

  }

  .flex-item {

    width: 100%;

    font-size: 18px;

    padding: 10px;

  }

}


/* Hide element on mobile */

@media (max-width: 767px) {

  .desktop-only {

    display: none;

  }

}
```

2. Update index.html to include an element with the desktop-only class.

Example HTML (index.html):

```
<div class="flex-container">

    <div class="flex-item">Item 1</div>

    <div class="flex-item">Item 2</div>

    <div class="flex-item">Item 3</div>

    <div class="desktop-only">This content only shows on desktop.</div>

</div>
```

3. Save both files and open index.html in your browser. Resize the browser window to see the responsive behavior in action.

Experiment with the breakpoints to see how the design adapts.

Lesson 17 Exercises: Practicing Responsive Design with Media Queries

In this lesson, you'll use media queries to adjust layouts and styles based on screen size.

Exercise 1: Setting Up a Basic Media Query

1. **Objective**: Apply different styles on smaller screens.

2. **Steps**:

   o In styles.css, add a media query to target screens with a maximum width of 600px:

```
@media (max-width: 600px) {

  body {

    background-color: #f0f8ff;

  }

}
```

   o Change the background color to #f0f8ff when the screen width is 600px or smaller.

3. **Expected Output**: On smaller screens, the background color of the page should change.

Exercise 2: Stacking Flex Items on Small Screens

1. **Objective**: Use media queries to change the flex layout for smaller screens.

2. **Steps**:

   o In styles.css, add a media query targeting screens with a maximum width of 600px.

- Inside the media query, set flex-direction: column; for .flex-container to stack items vertically.

3. **Expected Output**: When the screen width is 600px or less, the items should stack vertically instead of aligning in a row.

Exercise 3: Adjusting Font Size for Different Screen Sizes

1. **Objective**: Use media queries to change font sizes for readability on smaller screens.

2. **Steps**:

- Add a media query to target screens with a maximum width of 600px.

- Inside the media query, set a smaller font size (e.g., font-size: 14px;) for <h1> elements.

3. **Expected Output**: The <h1> font size should decrease on smaller screens, making the text more readable.

Exercise 4: Hiding Elements on Mobile

1. **Objective**: Hide elements that aren't necessary on smaller screens.

2. **Steps**:

- In index.html, add a <div class="sidebar">Sidebar Content</div> inside the <main> section.

- In styles.css, add a media query to hide the .sidebar when the screen width is 600px or smaller:

```
@media (max-width: 600px) {

  .sidebar {

    display: none;

  }
```

}

3. **Expected Output:** The sidebar should be hidden when the screen is 600px or smaller.

Lesson 18: CSS Grid Layout Basics

CSS Grid is a layout system that allows you to create two-dimensional layouts (rows and columns) and is very useful for designing more structured and responsive layouts.

1. Setting Up a Grid Container

To start with CSS Grid, apply display: grid; to a container. The direct children of this container become **grid items**.

```
.grid-container {

    display: grid;

}
```

2. Defining Columns and Rows with grid-template-columns and grid-template-rows

The grid-template-columns and grid-template-rows properties define the number of columns and rows in the grid, as well as their sizes.

Example:

```
.grid-container {

    display: grid;

    grid-template-columns: 1fr 1fr 1fr; /* Three equal-width columns */

    grid-template-rows: 100px 200px; /* Two rows with different heights */

}
```

- **fr (fraction)**: Distributes available space proportionally.
- **px, %, em**: You can also use fixed units like pixels or percentages.

3. Adding Gaps between Rows and Columns

The gap property adds space between rows and columns. You can also use row-gap and column-gap separately.

```
.grid-container {

   gap: 10px; /* 10px gap between both rows and columns */

}
```

4. Positioning Items within the Grid

Grid items can span multiple rows or columns using grid-column and grid-row properties.

Example:

```
.grid-item-1 {

   grid-column: 1 / 3; /* Spans from column 1 to 3 */

   grid-row: 1 / 2; /* Spans from row 1 to 2 */

}
```

5. Using repeat() and auto-fit for Responsive Layouts

The repeat() function and auto-fit keyword help create flexible layouts that automatically adjust based on screen size.

Example:

```
.grid-container {

   display: grid;

   grid-template-columns: repeat(auto-fit, minmax(150px, 1fr)); /* Columns adjust based on screen size */

}
```

Practice Task

1. Update your styles.css file to create a basic grid layout with multiple rows and columns.

Example CSS File (styles.css):

```css
/* Grid Container */
.grid-container {
    display: grid;
    grid-template-columns: 1fr 1fr 1fr; /* Three equal columns */
    grid-template-rows: 150px 150px; /* Two equal rows */
    gap: 10px; /* 10px space between items */
    padding: 20px;
    background-color: #f0f8ff;
}

/* Grid Items */
.grid-item {
    background-color: #3498db;
    color: white;
    display: flex;
    justify-content: center;
    align-items: center;
    font-size: 18px;
}
```

```css
/* Make Item 1 span two columns */

.grid-item-1 {

  grid-column: 1 / 3;

}


/* Make Item 4 span two rows */

.grid-item-4 {

  grid-row: 1 / 3;

}
```

2. Add the following HTML to index.html to create the grid layout.

Example HTML (index.html):

```html
<div class="grid-container">

  <div class="grid-item grid-item-1">Item 1</div>

  <div class="grid-item">Item 2</div>

  <div class="grid-item">Item 3</div>

  <div class="grid-item grid-item-4">Item 4</div>

  <div class="grid-item">Item 5</div>

  <div class="grid-item">Item 6</div>

</div>
```

3. Save both files and open index.html in your browser to see the grid in action.

Experiment by changing the column and row spans, and try using auto-fit with minmax() to make the grid responsive.

Lesson 18 Exercises: Practicing CSS Grid Layout

In this lesson, you'll practice using CSS Grid to create structured, responsive layouts.

Exercise 1: Setting Up a Basic Grid Layout

1. **Objective**: Create a grid layout with multiple columns and rows.

2. **Steps**:

   - In index.html, add a <div class="grid-container"> with six child <div> elements inside, each containing text like "Item 1", "Item 2", etc.

   - In styles.css, add:

```
.grid-container {

  display: grid;

  grid-template-columns: 1fr 1fr 1fr; /* Three equal-width columns */

  gap: 10px; /* Space between grid items */

}
.grid-container div {

  background-color: #3498db;

  color: white;

  padding: 20px;

  text-align: center;

}
```

3. **Expected Output**: The items should be arranged in a three-column grid layout with equal spacing between them.

Exercise 2: Using Grid Rows and Columns with repeat()

1. **Objective**: Simplify the grid structure using repeat().

2. **Steps**:

     o   In styles.css, replace grid-template-columns: 1fr 1fr 1fr; with grid-template-columns: repeat(3, 1fr);.

3. **Expected Output**: The layout should look the same, but your CSS code is now more concise.

Exercise 3: Making Items Span Multiple Columns or Rows

1. **Objective**: Make certain items span multiple columns or rows.

2. **Steps**:

     o   In styles.css, add:

```
.grid-container div:nth-child(1) {
   grid-column: span 2; /* Span first item across two columns */
}
.grid-container div:nth-child(2) {
   grid-row: span 2; /* Span second item across two rows */
}
```

3. **Expected Output**: The first item should span two columns, and the second item should span two rows, creating a more dynamic layout.

Exercise 4: Creating a Responsive Grid Layout

1. **Objective**: Use grid properties to make the layout responsive.

2. **Steps**:

o   In styles.css, add a media query for screens with a
maximum width of 600px:

```css
@media (max-width: 600px) {

  .grid-container {

    grid-template-columns: 1fr; /* Single column layout on small screens */

  }

}
```

3. **Expected Output**: On smaller screens, the grid should change to a
single-column layout, stacking the items vertically.

Lesson 19: Styling Forms with CSS

Forms are essential for user interaction on websites, and styling them can significantly improve the user experience. We'll explore ways to style form elements like input fields, labels, buttons, and more.

1. Basic Styling for Form Elements

Let's start by giving some basic styles to the form elements to make them more visually appealing.

Example:

```
/* Form Container */
form {
    max-width: 500px;
    margin: auto;
    padding: 20px;
    border: 1px solid #ddd;
    background-color: #f9f9f9;
    border-radius: 8px;
}


/* Labels */
label {
    display: block;
    margin-bottom: 5px;
    font-weight: bold;
    color: #333;
}
```

```css
/* Input Fields */
input[type="text"],
input[type="email"],
textarea {
    width: 100%;
    padding: 10px;
    margin-bottom: 15px;
    border: 1px solid #ccc;
    border-radius: 4px;
    font-size: 16px;
}

/* Submit Button */
button[type="submit"] {
    width: 100%;
    padding: 10px;
    background-color: #3498db;
    color: white;
    border: none;
    border-radius: 4px;
    font-size: 16px;
    cursor: pointer;
}
```

```
button[type="submit"]:hover {

   background-color: #2980b9;

}
```

2. Styling Focused and Hover States

Using :focus and :hover states can enhance user experience by highlighting fields when users interact with them.

Example:

```
input[type="text"]:focus,

input[type="email"]:focus,

textarea:focus {

   border-color: #3498db;

   box-shadow: 0 0 5px rgba(52, 152, 219, 0.5);

}
```

3. Styling Different Input Types

Different input types, such as checkboxes and radio buttons, can be styled for consistency. You can also use custom styles for these elements if needed.

Example:

```
/* Checkbox and Radio Buttons */

input[type="checkbox"],

input[type="radio"] {

   margin-right: 5px;

}
```

4. Placeholder Text Styling

You can style the placeholder text within input fields for a consistent look.

Example:

input::placeholder,

textarea::placeholder {

  color: #aaa;

  font-style: italic;

}

Practice Task

1. Update your styles.css file to include styles for a form, its input fields, labels, and buttons.

Example CSS File (styles.css):

/* Form Container */

form {

  max-width: 500px;

  margin: auto;

  padding: 20px;

  border: 1px solid #ddd;

  background-color: #f9f9f9;

  border-radius: 8px;

}

/* Labels */

```css
label {
    display: block;
    margin-bottom: 5px;
    font-weight: bold;
    color: #333;
}

/* Input Fields */
input[type="text"],
input[type="email"],
textarea {
    width: 100%;
    padding: 10px;
    margin-bottom: 15px;
    border: 1px solid #ccc;
    border-radius: 4px;
    font-size: 16px;
}

/* Placeholder Text */
input::placeholder,
textarea::placeholder {
    color: #aaa;
    font-style: italic;
}
```

```css
/* Submit Button */
button[type="submit"] {
    width: 100%;
    padding: 10px;
    background-color: #3498db;
    color: white;
    border: none;
    border-radius: 4px;
    font-size: 16px;
    cursor: pointer;
}

button[type="submit"]:hover {
    background-color: #2980b9;
}

/* Focused Input Fields */
input[type="text"]:focus,
input[type="email"]:focus,
textarea:focus {
    border-color: #3498db;
    box-shadow: 0 0 5px rgba(52, 152, 219, 0.5);
}
```

2. Add the following HTML code for a sample form to index.html.

Example HTML (index.html):

```html
<form action="/submit-form" method="POST">

  <label for="name">Name</label>

  <input type="text" id="name" name="name" placeholder="Enter your name">


  <label for="email">Email</label>

  <input type="email" id="email" name="email" placeholder="Enter your email">


  <label for="message">Message</label>

  <textarea id="message" name="message" rows="4" placeholder="Enter your message"></textarea>


  <button type="submit">Submit</button>
</form>
```

3. Save both files and open index.html in your browser. Observe how the form styling improves the overall user experience.

Experiment with different colors, border styles, and padding to see how each affects the form's appearance.

Lesson 19 Exercises: Practicing Form Styling

In this lesson, you'll practice using CSS to style form elements for a clean and user-friendly appearance.

Exercise 1: Basic Form Styling

1. **Objective**: Apply basic styling to form elements.

2. **Steps**:

   o In your index.html file, add a <form> with the following fields:

      ▪ An <input> for "Name"

      ▪ An <input> for "Email"

      ▪ A <textarea> for "Message"

      ▪ A <button> to submit the form

   o In styles.css, add styles to:

      ▪ Set width: 100%; for the inputs and text area

      ▪ Add padding: 10px; and margin-bottom: 15px;

3. **Expected Output**: The form inputs and text area should fill the width of the form container and have padding and spacing for a more comfortable layout.

Exercise 2: Styling the Submit Button

1. **Objective**: Style the submit button to make it visually appealing.

2. **Steps**:

   o In styles.css, add styles to the submit button:

```
button {
  background-color: #3498db;
```

```
  color: white;

  padding: 10px 20px;

  border: none;

  border-radius: 5px;

  cursor: pointer;

}

button:hover {

  background-color: #2980b9;

}
```

3. **Expected Output**: The button should have a blue background with white text, rounded corners, and a hover effect that changes its color.

Exercise 3: Adding Focus Styles to Inputs

1. **Objective**: Style input fields when they're focused for better user experience.

2. **Steps**:

   o In styles.css, add a focus style for the inputs and text area:

```
input:focus, textarea:focus {

  border-color: #3498db;

  box-shadow: 0 0 5px rgba(52, 152, 219, 0.5);

  outline: none;

}
```

3. **Expected Output**: When users click into an input or text area, a blue border and soft shadow should appear, helping users see where they are in the form.

Exercise 4: Aligning Labels with Form Fields

1. **Objective**: Ensure labels and form fields are consistently aligned.

2. **Steps**:

   - Wrap each input and its corresponding label in a <div class="form-group">.

   - In styles.css, add styles to .form-group to add spacing between label-field pairs:

```css
.form-group {

   margin-bottom: 15px;

}

label {

   display: block;

   font-weight: bold;

   margin-bottom: 5px;

}
```

3. **Expected Output**: Labels should appear above each form field with spacing between label-field pairs for better readability.

Lesson 20: Transitions and Animations

CSS transitions and animations enhance the user experience by adding movement and interactivity to elements. Transitions create smooth changes from one style to another, while animations provide more control over complex movements.

1. CSS Transitions

Transitions allow you to change an element's style gradually over time, triggered by user actions like hover or click.

- **Properties of a Transition**:

    - **transition-property**: Specifies the property to transition (e.g., color, background-color).

    - **transition-duration**: Specifies how long the transition takes.

    - **transition-timing-function**: Defines the speed curve (e.g., ease, linear, ease-in, ease-out).

    - **transition-delay**: Sets a delay before the transition starts.

Example:

```
.button {
    background-color: #3498db;
    color: white;
    padding: 10px 20px;
    border: none;
    border-radius: 5px;
    transition: background-color 0.3s ease, transform 0.3s ease;
}
```

```
.button:hover {

    background-color: #2980b9;

    transform: scale(1.1); /* Slightly enlarges the button */

}
```

2. CSS Animations

CSS animations are more flexible, allowing you to define complex sequences. They use @keyframes to specify a set of styles at various stages of the animation.

- **animation-name**: Refers to the @keyframes animation.

- **animation-duration**: Specifies how long the animation lasts.

- **animation-timing-function**: Defines the speed curve.

- **animation-delay**: Sets a delay before the animation starts.

- **animation-iteration-count**: Sets the number of times the animation repeats (e.g., infinite for endless looping).

Example:

```
@keyframes fadeIn {

  from {

    opacity: 0;

  }

  to {

    opacity: 1;

  }

}
```

```
.fade-in {

  opacity: 0; /* Initial opacity */

  animation: fadeIn 2s ease-in-out forwards;

}
```

In this example, the .fade-in class will gradually fade in over 2 seconds.

3. Applying Animations to Different Elements

You can use animations to create effects like color changes, slide-in elements, bouncing effects, and more.

Example: Slide-in Animation:

```
@keyframes slideIn {

  from {

    transform: translateX(-100%);

  }

  to {

    transform: translateX(0);

  }

}


.slide-in {

  animation: slideIn 0.5s ease-out;

}
```

Practice Task

1. Add the following CSS code to styles.css to practice using transitions and animations.

Example CSS File (styles.css):

```css
/* Transition Example */
.button {
  background-color: #3498db;
  color: white;
  padding: 10px 20px;
  border: none;
  border-radius: 5px;
  transition: background-color 0.3s ease, transform 0.3s ease;
}

.button:hover {
  background-color: #2980b9;
  transform: scale(1.1); /* Enlarges on hover */
}

/* Fade-in Animation */
@keyframes fadeIn {
  from {
    opacity: 0;
  }
  to {
    opacity: 1;
  }
}
```

```css
  }

  .fade-in {
    opacity: 0;
    animation: fadeIn 2s ease-in-out forwards;
  }

  /* Slide-in Animation */
  @keyframes slideIn {
    from {
      transform: translateX(-100%);
    }
    to {
      transform: translateX(0);
    }
  }

  .slide-in {
    animation: slideIn 0.5s ease-out;
  }
```

2. Add the following HTML to index.html to test transitions and animations.

Example HTML (index.html):

```
<button class="button">Hover Me!</button>


<div class="fade-in" style="margin-top: 20px;">

  <p>This text fades in on load.</p>

</div>


<div class="slide-in" style="margin-top: 20px;">

  <p>This text slides in from the left.</p>

</div>
```

3. Save both files and open index.html in your browser. Try hovering over the button and observe the fade-in and slide-in animations.

Experiment by changing the timing and properties for different effects.

Lesson 20 Exercises: Practicing CSS Transitions and Animations

In this lesson, you'll work with transitions and animations to create smooth, interactive effects on your page.

Exercise 1: Adding a Transition Effect to a Button

1. **Objective**: Use CSS transitions to create a smooth color change on hover.

2. **Steps**:

   o   In styles.css, add a transition effect to your submit button:

```css
button {

  background-color: #3498db;

  color: white;

  padding: 10px 20px;

  border: none;

  border-radius: 5px;

  cursor: pointer;

  transition: background-color 0.3s ease;

}
button:hover {

  background-color: #2980b9;

}
```

3. **Expected Output**: When hovering over the button, the background color should smoothly transition to a darker shade.

Exercise 2: Applying a Fade-in Animation

1. **Objective**: Create a fade-in effect on a content section.

2. **Steps**:

   o In styles.css, define an animation named fadeIn:

```css
@keyframes fadeIn {

  from { opacity: 0; }

  to { opacity: 1; }

}
```

   o Apply this animation to a section of your choice, with animation: fadeIn 2s ease-in-out;.

3. **Expected Output**: The content section should fade in over 2 seconds when the page loads.

Exercise 3: Creating a Hover Scale Animation

1. **Objective**: Add a scale effect on hover for an image or card.

2. **Steps**:

   o In styles.css, select an image or card element and add:

```css
.card {

  transition: transform 0.3s ease;

}
.card:hover {

  transform: scale(1.05);

}
```

3. **Expected Output**: When hovering over the image or card, it should slightly enlarge, creating a zoom-in effect.

Exercise 4: Adding a Slide-in Animation

1. **Objective**: Make an element slide in from the left when the page loads.

2. **Steps**:

   o   Define an animation in styles.css:

```css
@keyframes slideIn {
  from { transform: translateX(-100%); }
  to { transform: translateX(0); }
}
```

   o   Apply the slideIn animation to an element, with animation: slideIn 1s ease-out;.

3. **Expected Output**: The element should slide in from the left side of the screen over 1 second when the page loads.

Lesson 21: SVG and Icon Integration

Scalable Vector Graphics (SVG) are resolution-independent graphics that can be styled and animated with CSS, making them ideal for responsive designs. Icons, typically SVG or font-based, are commonly used for web interfaces.

1. What is SVG?

SVG is an XML-based format for creating vector graphics. SVG files are scalable and remain crisp on all screen sizes and resolutions, making them perfect for icons, logos, and illustrations.

Example of Basic SVG Code:

```
<svg width="100" height="100">

  <circle cx="50" cy="50" r="40" fill="blue" />

</svg>
```

- **<svg>**: Defines an SVG container. The width and height attributes set the SVG's dimensions.
- **<circle>**: Creates a circle. cx and cy set the circle's center, r sets the radius, and fill defines the color.

2. Inline SVG

You can place SVG code directly in your HTML, allowing you to style and animate it with CSS.

Example of Inline SVG:

```
<svg width="100" height="100" class="my-icon">

  <circle cx="50" cy="50" r="40" fill="blue" />

</svg>
```

Styling SVG with CSS:

```
.my-icon {

  fill: red; /* Changes the color */

  transition: fill 0.3s ease;

}


.my-icon:hover {

  fill: green; /* Changes color on hover */

}
```

3. Embedding SVG Files

You can also reference external SVG files using the <img> tag or as a CSS background image.

Using <img>:

```
<img src="icon.svg" alt="An icon">
```

Using CSS Background:

```
.icon-background {

  width: 50px;

  height: 50px;

  background-image: url('icon.svg');

  background-size: cover;

}
```

4. Font Icons (e.g., Font Awesome)

Font-based icons are another popular way to add icons to your website. Libraries like **Font Awesome** provide an extensive collection of icons. These icons are inserted as text elements, making them easy to size and color with CSS.

Example with Font Awesome (assuming you have Font Awesome linked):

```
<link rel="stylesheet" href="https://cdnjs.cloudflare.com/ajax/libs/font-
awesome/6.0.0-beta3/css/all.min.css">
```

```
<i class="fas fa-camera"></i>
```

Styling Font Icons:

```
i {
    font-size: 24px;
    color: #3498db;
}
```

```
i:hover {
    color: #2980b9;
}
```

5. SVG Animation

You can animate SVG elements with CSS, adding effects like scaling, rotating, and changing colors.

Example:

```
<svg width="100" height="100" class="animated-icon">
    <circle cx="50" cy="50" r="40" fill="blue" />
</svg>
```

css

Code kopiëren

```css
.animated-icon {
    transition: transform 0.3s ease;
}


.animated-icon:hover {
    transform: scale(1.2); /* Enlarges on hover */
}
```

Practice Task

1. Add the following SVG and Font Awesome icons to your HTML file.

Example HTML (index.html):

```html
<!-- Inline SVG Icon -->

<svg width="100" height="100" class="my-icon">

  <circle cx="50" cy="50" r="40" fill="blue" />

</svg>


<!-- Font Awesome Icon -->

<link rel="stylesheet" href="https://cdnjs.cloudflare.com/ajax/libs/font-awesome/6.0.0-beta3/css/all.min.css">

<i class="fas fa-camera"></i>
```

2. Add the following styles to styles.css to style and animate the icons.

Example CSS (styles.css):

```css
/* Inline SVG Icon Styling */
.my-icon {
    fill: #3498db;
    transition: fill 0.3s ease, transform 0.3s ease;
}


.my-icon:hover {
    fill: #2980b9;
    transform: scale(1.2);
}


/* Font Awesome Icon Styling */
i {
    font-size: 24px;
    color: #3498db;
    margin-top: 20px;
}


i:hover {
    color: #2980b9;
}
```

3. Save both files and open index.html in your browser to test the SVG and icon styling.

Experiment with different SVG shapes and icon libraries to add variety.

Lesson 21 Exercises: Working with SVGs and Icons

In this lesson, you'll practice adding SVG graphics and icons to your HTML page for better visual elements.

Exercise 1: Embedding an Inline SVG

1. **Objective**: Add an SVG directly within the HTML.

2. **Steps**:

   o   In index.html, add an SVG below your main heading:

```
<svg width="100" height="100">

  <circle cx="50" cy="50" r="40" fill="#3498db" />

</svg>
```

3. **Expected Output**: You should see a blue circle displayed under your main heading.

Exercise 2: Styling an Inline SVG with CSS

1. **Objective**: Apply CSS to change the color of an SVG on hover.

2. **Steps**:

   o   Add a class="icon" to your SVG.

   o   In styles.css, add styles to .icon:

```
.icon {

  transition: fill 0.3s ease;

}

.icon:hover {

  fill: #2980b9;
```

}

3. **Expected Output**: When hovering over the SVG, the circle's color should change smoothly.

Exercise 3: Adding an External SVG Image

1. **Objective**: Use an external SVG as an image.

2. **Steps**:

   o   Save an SVG file in your project folder (e.g., icon.svg).

   o   In index.html, add the SVG using the <img> tag:

```
<img src="icon.svg" alt="An icon image">
```

3. **Expected Output**: The external SVG should display on your page as an image.

Exercise 4: Adding a Font Icon (e.g., Font Awesome)

1. **Objective**: Use a font-based icon library like Font Awesome.

2. **Steps**:

   o   Add the Font Awesome CDN to the <head> section of your index.html:

```
<link rel="stylesheet" href="https://cdnjs.cloudflare.com/ajax/libs/font-awesome/6.0.0-beta3/css/all.min.css">
```

   o   In the body, add an icon using <i>:

```
<i class="fas fa-camera"></i>
```

   o   In styles.css, style the icon with font-size: 24px; and color: #3498db;.

3. **Expected Output**: A camera icon from Font Awesome should display on your page with the specified size and color.

Lesson 22: Advanced Form Features and Validation

HTML5 provides several built-in features for form validation, which help ensure users enter information in the correct format before submitting the form. This includes validation attributes, advanced input types, and feedback messages.

1. New HTML5 Input Types

HTML5 introduces various input types to make data collection easier and more accurate:

- **type="email"**: Requires a valid email format.

<input type="email" name="email" placeholder="Enter your email" required>

- **type="url"**: Requires a valid URL format.

<input type="url" name="website" placeholder="Enter your website URL">

- **type="number"**: Allows only numbers within a specified range.

<input type="number" name="age" min="1" max="100">

- **type="date"**: Opens a date picker.

<input type="date" name="birthdate">

- **type="tel"**: For telephone numbers.

<input type="tel" name="phone" placeholder="Enter your phone number">

2. Form Validation Attributes

HTML5 offers several attributes to improve validation:

- **required**: Ensures the field must be filled out.

<input type="text" name="username" required>

- **pattern**: Requires the input to match a regular expression.

```
<input type="text" name="zipcode" pattern="\d{5}" placeholder="Enter 5-
digit ZIP code">
```

- **min, max, step**: Define a numeric range and step intervals.

```
<input type="number" name="quantity" min="1" max="10" step="1">
```

- **maxlength**: Sets the maximum length of input.

```
<input type="text" name="username" maxlength="15">
```

3. Placeholder and Autofocus

- **placeholder**: Provides a hint to the user about the expected value.

```
<input type="text" name="city" placeholder="Enter your city">
```

- **autofocus**: Automatically focuses on an input field when the page loads.

```
<input type="text" name="firstname" autofocus>
```

4. Form Validation with CSS

You can style valid and invalid inputs using CSS pseudo-classes:

- **:valid**: Styles valid inputs.
- **:invalid**: Styles invalid inputs.

Example:

```
input:valid {
    border-color: green;
}


input:invalid {
```

```
  border-color: red;

}
```

5. Custom Validation Messages

You can use the setCustomValidity() function in JavaScript to display custom messages when validation fails.

Example:

```html
<input type="email" id="email" placeholder="Enter your email" required>

<script>

  const email = document.getElementById('email');

  email.addEventListener('input', function () {

    if (email.validity.typeMismatch) {

      email.setCustomValidity('Please enter a valid email address.');

    } else {

      email.setCustomValidity('');

    }

  });

</script>
```

Practice Task

1. Add the following code to index.html to create a form with various input types and validation.

Example HTML (index.html):

```html
<form action="/submit-form" method="POST">

  <label for="email">Email:</label>
```

```html
    <input type="email" id="email" name="email" placeholder="Enter your
email" required>


    <label for="website">Website:</label>

    <input type="url" id="website" name="website" placeholder="Enter your
website URL">


    <label for="birthdate">Birthdate:</label>

    <input type="date" id="birthdate" name="birthdate">


    <label for="quantity">Quantity (1-10):</label>

    <input type="number" id="quantity" name="quantity" min="1" max="10"
required>


    <label for="zipcode">ZIP Code:</label>

    <input type="text" id="zipcode" name="zipcode" pattern="\d{5}"
placeholder="Enter 5-digit ZIP code" required>


    <button type="submit">Submit</button>
</form>
```

2. Add some basic CSS to styles.css to style valid and invalid inputs.

Example CSS (styles.css):

```css
input:valid {

   border-color: green;

}
```

```css
input:invalid {
    border-color: red;
}

button[type="submit"] {
    margin-top: 10px;
    padding: 10px;
    background-color: #3498db;
    color: white;
    border: none;
    border-radius: 4px;
    cursor: pointer;
}

button[type="submit"]:hover {
    background-color: #2980b9;
}
```

3. Save both files and open index.html in your browser. Test the form by entering valid and invalid data to see the validation effects.

Try experimenting with different input types and validation requirements.

Lesson 22 Exercises: Practicing Advanced Form Features and Validation

In this lesson, you'll work with HTML5 form validation attributes and use JavaScript to create custom validation messages.

Exercise 1: Using Required Fields

1. **Objective**: Ensure users cannot submit a form without filling in specific fields.

2. **Steps**:

   o In your index.html form, add the required attribute to the "Name" and "Email" inputs.

   o Try submitting the form without filling out the required fields to see the browser's default error messages.

3. **Expected Output**: The form should not submit, and you should see a browser-provided message indicating that the fields are required.

Exercise 2: Validating an Email Format

1. **Objective**: Use HTML5 validation to check for a properly formatted email.

2. **Steps**:

   o In the "Email" input field, ensure the type attribute is set to email.

   o Try entering an incorrectly formatted email (e.g., user@domain) and attempt to submit the form.

3. **Expected Output**: The browser should display an error message indicating that the email format is incorrect.

Exercise 3: Adding Pattern Validation for a Phone Number

1. **Objective**: Use the pattern attribute to validate a phone number format.

2. **Steps**:

   o Add a new input field for "Phone Number" in your form.

   o Set type="tel" and add pattern="\d{10}" to only accept 10-digit phone numbers.

   o Try entering a phone number in a different format (e.g., 123-456-789) and attempt to submit the form.

3. **Expected Output**: The form should not submit, and the browser should indicate that the phone number format is invalid.

Exercise 4: Custom Validation Message with JavaScript

1. **Objective**: Provide a custom validation message for an incorrectly formatted email.

2. **Steps**:

   o Add the following JavaScript to index.html within a <script> tag:

```
const emailField = document.getElementById('email');

emailField.addEventListener('input', function () {

  if (emailField.validity.typeMismatch) {

    emailField.setCustomValidity('Please enter a valid email address.');

  } else {

    emailField.setCustomValidity('');

  }

});
```

- o   Test the form by entering an invalid email format to see the custom message.

3.   **Expected Output**: Instead of the default message, you should see "Please enter a valid email address" if the email format is incorrect.

Lesson 23: CSS Variables and Custom Properties

CSS variables, also known as custom properties, allow you to define reusable values, making it easier to manage and update styles consistently throughout your CSS. They improve maintainability and make it simple to implement design changes across your site.

1. Defining CSS Variables

CSS variables are defined with a -- prefix and can be assigned any value. They are typically declared within the :root selector to make them globally accessible across your styles.

Example:

:root {

  --primary-color: #3498db;

  --secondary-color: #2980b9;

  --font-size-large: 24px;

}

In this example:

- --primary-color and --secondary-color store color values.

- --font-size-large stores a font size.

2. Using CSS Variables

To use a CSS variable, reference it with the var() function.

Example:

h1 {

  color: var(--primary-color);

```css
  font-size: var(--font-size-large);

}


button {

  background-color: var(--secondary-color);

  color: white;

  padding: 10px;

}
```

3. Updating Variables for Theming

CSS variables make it easy to create themes by updating variable values. For example, you can change colors for light and dark themes by redefining variables.

Example:

```css
/* Light Theme */

:root {

  --background-color: #ffffff;

  --text-color: #333333;

}


/* Dark Theme */

body.dark-theme {

  --background-color: #333333;

  --text-color: #ffffff;

}
```

```css
/* Applying Variables */

body {

  background-color: var(--background-color);

  color: var(--text-color);

}
```

You can toggle the dark-theme class on the <body> element to switch between themes.

4. Using Variables with JavaScript

CSS variables can also be manipulated with JavaScript to create interactive themes or dynamic styling. You can access and modify custom properties through JavaScript using style.setProperty().

Example:

```html
<button onclick="toggleTheme()">Toggle Theme</button>


<script>
  function toggleTheme() {

    const root = document.documentElement;

    if (root.style.getPropertyValue('--background-color') === '#ffffff') {

      root.style.setProperty('--background-color', '#333333');

      root.style.setProperty('--text-color', '#ffffff');

    } else {

      root.style.setProperty('--background-color', '#ffffff');

      root.style.setProperty('--text-color', '#333333');

    }

  }
```

```
</script>
```

Practice Task

1. Add the following variables to styles.css to set up a basic color scheme.

Example CSS (styles.css):

```css
:root {

  --primary-color: #3498db;

  --secondary-color: #2980b9;

  --background-color: #f9f9f9;

  --text-color: #333333;

  --font-size-large: 24px;

}


body {

  background-color: var(--background-color);

  color: var(--text-color);

  font-family: Arial, sans-serif;

}


h1 {

  color: var(--primary-color);

  font-size: var(--font-size-large);

}
```

```
button {
    background-color: var(--secondary-color);
    color: white;
    padding: 10px 20px;
    border: none;
    border-radius: 5px;
    cursor: pointer;
    transition: background-color 0.3s ease;
}

button:hover {
    background-color: var(--primary-color);
}
```

2. Add the following HTML to index.html to test the styling with a button.

Example HTML (index.html):

```
<h1>CSS Variables and Custom Properties</h1>
<p>This page uses CSS variables for consistent styling.</p>

<button onclick="toggleTheme()">Toggle Theme</button>

<script>
```

```
function toggleTheme() {
  const root = document.documentElement;
  if (root.style.getPropertyValue('--background-color') === '#f9f9f9') {
    root.style.setProperty('--background-color', '#333333');
    root.style.setProperty('--text-color', '#ffffff');
  } else {
    root.style.setProperty('--background-color', '#f9f9f9');
    root.style.setProperty('--text-color', '#333333');
  }
}
</script>
```

3. Save both files and open index.html in your browser. Click the "Toggle Theme" button to see how the background and text colors switch between light and dark themes.

Experiment with different variable values and add more variables for fonts, spacing, or other properties.

Lesson 23 Exercises: Practicing CSS Variables and Custom Properties

In this lesson, you'll define and use CSS variables to streamline styling and make it easier to manage design changes.

Exercise 1: Defining and Using CSS Variables

1. **Objective**: Define and apply CSS variables for primary colors.

2. **Steps**:

   o In styles.css, add the following variables in the :root selector:

```
:root {

  --primary-color: #3498db;

  --secondary-color: #2980b9;

  --font-color: #333333;

}
```

   o Apply var(--primary-color) as the background color for your main heading (h1), var(--secondary-color) as the color for <h2> elements, and var(--font-color) as the text color for paragraphs.

3. **Expected Output**: Your main heading should have a primary background color, <h2> elements should use the secondary color, and paragraphs should display in the specified font color.

Exercise 2: Using Variables for Font Sizes

1. **Objective**: Use variables to control font sizes.

2. **Steps**:

   o Add the following font size variables to :root in styles.css:

```
:root {

  --font-size-large: 24px;

  --font-size-medium: 18px;

  --font-size-small: 14px;

}
```

- Apply var(--font-size-large) to <h1>, var(--font-size-medium) to <h2>, and var(--font-size-small) to <p> elements.

3. **Expected Output**: The headings and paragraphs should now display with different font sizes based on the defined variables.

Exercise 3: Creating a Theme Switch with JavaScript

1. **Objective**: Use JavaScript to toggle between light and dark themes.

2. **Steps**:

   - In styles.css, add variables for background and text color in both light and dark themes:

```
:root {

  --background-color: #ffffff;

  --text-color: #333333;

}
.dark-theme {

  --background-color: #333333;

  --text-color: #ffffff;

}
body {

  background-color: var(--background-color);

  color: var(--text-color);
```

```
}
```

- In index.html, add a button with onclick="toggleTheme()" and label it "Toggle Theme".
- Add the following JavaScript in a <script> tag to toggle themes:

```
function toggleTheme() {

  document.body.classList.toggle('dark-theme');

}
```

3. **Expected Output**: When you click the "Toggle Theme" button, the background and text colors should switch between light and dark themes.

Lesson 24: CSS Pseudo-classes and Pseudo-elements

Pseudo-classes and pseudo-elements allow you to style elements based on their state, position, or specific parts, enhancing the interactivity and visual detail of your web design.

1. Pseudo-classes

Pseudo-classes style elements based on their state, such as when they're being hovered over or clicked. They're added after the selector with a colon (:).

- **:hover**: Styles an element when the user hovers over it.

```
button:hover {

  background-color: #2980b9;

}
```

- **:focus**: Styles an element when it's focused, often used for inputs.

```
input:focus {

  border-color: #3498db;

}
```

- **:nth-child()**: Styles elements based on their order in a parent. You can specify positions like 2, odd, or even.

```
li:nth-child(odd) {

  background-color: #f0f8ff;

}
```

- **:first-child and :last-child**: Styles only the first or last child element within a parent.

```
p:first-child {

  font-weight: bold;
```

```
}
```

```
p:last-child {

    color: #3498db;

}
```

2. Pseudo-elements

Pseudo-elements style specific parts of an element, such as the first letter or line. They're added with a double colon (::), though some browsers also support a single colon.

- **::first-line**: Styles the first line of text in a block.

```
p::first-line {

    font-weight: bold;

}
```

- **::first-letter**: Styles the first letter of a block of text, often used for decorative purposes.

```
p::first-letter {

    font-size: 2em;

    color: #3498db;

}
```

- **::before and ::after**: Adds content before or after an element, useful for decorative icons or additional details. Use the content property to define what to add.

```
.quote::before {

    content: """;

    font-size: 2em;

    color: #3498db;
```

```
}


.quote::after {

  content: """;

  font-size: 2em;

  color: #3498db;

}
```

Practice Task

1. Add the following pseudo-class and pseudo-element styles to styles.css.

Example CSS (styles.css):

```
/* Button Hover */

button:hover {

  background-color: #2980b9;

  transform: scale(1.05);

}


/* Focused Input Field */

input:focus {

  border-color: #3498db;

  outline: none;

  box-shadow: 0 0 5px rgba(52, 152, 219, 0.5);

}
```

```css
/* Alternate List Item Colors */
li:nth-child(odd) {
    background-color: #f0f8ff;
}


li:nth-child(even) {
    background-color: #dcdcdc;
}


/* First Line and First Letter Styles */
p::first-line {
    font-weight: bold;
}


p::first-letter {
    font-size: 2em;
    color: #3498db;
}


/* Quote Style with Before and After */
.quote::before {
    content: """;
    font-size: 2em;
    color: #3498db;
```

```
}
```

```
.quote::after {
    content: "”";
    font-size: 2em;
    color: #3498db;
}
```

2. Add the following HTML to index.html to test the pseudo-classes and pseudo-elements.

Example HTML (index.html):

```
<button>Hover Me!</button>
```

```
<p class="quote">This is a quote with decorative quotation marks.</p>
```

```
<p>Lorem ipsum dolor sit amet, consectetur adipiscing elit. Praesent sit amet turpis ac nisi ultricies ultrices.</p>
```

```
<ul>
    <li>List item 1</li>
    <li>List item 2</li>
    <li>List item 3</li>
    <li>List item 4</li>
</ul>
```

3. Save both files and open index.html in your browser. Test the hover effect on the button, the focused state on an input (add one if needed), and observe how the list and paragraph styles look.

Try experimenting with other pseudo-classes like :nth-of-type() and pseudo-elements for specific design effects.

Lesson 24 Exercises: Practicing Pseudo-classes and Pseudo-elements

In this lesson, you'll work with pseudo-classes and pseudo-elements to style elements based on their state or specific parts.

Exercise 1: Applying Hover and Focus Styles

1. **Objective**: Use pseudo-classes to style elements on hover and focus.

2. **Steps**:

   o   In styles.css, add:

      ▪   A :hover style to buttons, changing their background color to #2980b9.

      ▪   A :focus style for input fields, changing their border color to #3498db.

3. **Expected Output**: Buttons should change color when hovered, and input fields should show a different border color when focused.

Exercise 2: Styling the First Child of a List

1. **Objective**: Use :first-child to style the first item in a list differently.

2. **Steps**:

   o   In index.html, add an unordered list with a few list items.

   o   In styles.css, add:

```
li:first-child {
  font-weight: bold;
  color: #3498db;
}
```

3. **Expected Output:** The first list item should appear bold and in blue.

Exercise 3: Using Pseudo-elements for Decorative Content

1. **Objective**: Add decorative content before and after an element using pseudo-elements.

2. **Steps:**

   - In index.html, add a <p class="quote">This is an inspirational quote.</p>.

   - In styles.css, add:

.quote::before {

  content: "“";

  font-size: 2em;

  color: #3498db;

}

.quote::after {

  content: "”";

  font-size: 2em;

  color: #3498db;

}

3. **Expected Output**: The quote paragraph should display with quotation marks around the text, styled with a larger font size and blue color.

Exercise 4: Styling the First Line and First Letter

1. **Objective**: Style the first line and first letter of a paragraph for emphasis.

2. **Steps**:

   o   In index.html, add a new paragraph with some text.

   o   In styles.css, add:

```
p::first-line {
  font-weight: bold;
}
p::first-letter {
  font-size: 2em;
  color: #2980b9;
}
```

3. **Expected Output**: The first line of the paragraph should be bold, and the first letter should appear larger and in blue.

Lesson 25: CSS Transformations

CSS transformations allow you to visually manipulate elements by rotating, scaling, skewing, or translating (moving) them. These transformations can be applied to elements to create engaging visual effects, and they work well in combination with transitions and animations.

1. The transform Property

The transform property is used to apply different types of transformations. Each transformation function affects an element in a unique way.

2. Transformation Types

- **Translate**: Moves an element horizontally, vertically, or both.

```
.box {

    transform: translate(50px, 100px); /* Moves 50px right and 100px down */

}
```

- **Scale**: Resizes an element. A value greater than 1 enlarges it, while a value between 0 and 1 shrinks it.

```
.box {

    transform: scale(1.5); /* Enlarges the element to 1.5 times its size */

}
```

- **Rotate**: Rotates an element by a specified angle, in degrees.

```
.box {

    transform: rotate(45deg); /* Rotates 45 degrees clockwise */

}
```

- **Skew**: Tilts an element horizontally, vertically, or both.

```
.box {
```

```
    transform: skew(20deg, 10deg); /* Skews 20 degrees on the X-axis and 10
degrees on the Y-axis */

}
```

3. Combining Transformations

You can combine multiple transformations by separating them with a space. They'll be applied in the order they're written.

Example:

```
.box {

    transform: translate(20px, 30px) scale(1.2) rotate(45deg);

}
```

4. Transform Origin

The transform-origin property sets the point from which the transformation occurs, usually specified as a percentage or keyword (e.g., top, left, center).

Example:

```
.box {

    transform-origin: center center; /* Default */

    transform: rotate(45deg);

}
```

5. Perspective and 3D Transformations

3D transformations create depth by adding perspective. Setting a perspective on the parent element affects child elements.

Example:

```
.container {
```

```
  perspective: 500px;

}
```

```
.box {

  transform: rotateY(45deg); /* Rotates around the Y-axis to create a 3D
effect */

}
```

Practice Task

1. Add the following transformation effects to styles.css for different
   visual effects.

Example CSS (styles.css):

```
/* Translation */

.translate-box {

  background-color: #3498db;

  color: white;

  padding: 20px;

  transform: translate(50px, 20px);

}
```

```
/* Scaling */

.scale-box {

  background-color: #2980b9;

  color: white;

  padding: 20px;
```

```css
    transform: scale(1.2);

    transition: transform 0.3s ease;

}


.scale-box:hover {

    transform: scale(1.5); /* Enlarges on hover */

}


/* Rotation */
.rotate-box {

    background-color: #27ae60;

    color: white;

    padding: 20px;

    transform: rotate(15deg);

    transition: transform 0.3s ease;

}


.rotate-box:hover {

    transform: rotate(45deg); /* Rotates further on hover */

}


/* Skew */
.skew-box {

    background-color: #f39c12;

    color: white;
```

```css
  padding: 20px;

  transform: skew(15deg, 10deg);

}


/* 3D Rotation with Perspective */

.container {

  perspective: 500px;

}


.rotate3d-box {

  background-color: #8e44ad;

  color: white;

  padding: 20px;

  transform: rotateY(45deg);

  transition: transform 0.5s ease;

}


.rotate3d-box:hover {

  transform: rotateY(90deg); /* Rotates to 90 degrees on hover */

}
```

2. Add the following HTML to index.html to test each transformation effect.

Example HTML (index.html):

```
<div class="translate-box">Translate Box</div>

<div class="scale-box">Scale Box (Hover to Scale Up)</div>

<div class="rotate-box">Rotate Box (Hover to Rotate)</div>

<div class="skew-box">Skew Box</div>


<div class="container">

  <div class="rotate3d-box">3D Rotate Box (Hover to Rotate)</div>

</div>
```

3. Save both files and open index.html in your browser. Test each box to see how the transformations affect its appearance and behavior.

Try combining transformations and adjusting the transform origin for different effects.

Lesson 25 Exercises: Practicing CSS Transformations

In this lesson, you'll work with the transform property to manipulate elements using translation, scaling, rotation, and skewing.

Exercise 1: Applying a Translation Transformation

1. **Objective**: Move an element from its original position using translate.

2. **Steps**:

   - In index.html, add a <div class="box">Translate Me</div>.

   - In styles.css, style .box with width: 100px;, height: 100px;, and background-color: #3498db;.

   - Add transform: translate(50px, 20px); to move the box 50px to the right and 20px down.

3. **Expected Output**: The box should appear shifted from its original position.

Exercise 2: Scaling an Element on Hover

1. **Objective**: Enlarge an element when hovered.

2. **Steps**:

   - In styles.css, add a scaling transformation to .box for the hover state:

```css
.box:hover {

  transform: scale(1.2);

}
```

3. **Expected Output**: When you hover over the box, it should enlarge by 20%.

Exercise 3: Rotating an Element

1. **Objective**: Rotate an element by a specific angle.

2. **Steps**:

   - In styles.css, add transform: rotate(45deg); to the .box class to rotate it 45 degrees.

3. **Expected Output**: The box should appear rotated 45 degrees from its original position.

Exercise 4: Skewing an Element

1. **Objective**: Tilt an element using the skew transformation.

2. **Steps**:

   - In styles.css, add another <div class="skew-box">Skew Me</div> to index.html with similar styling as .box.

   - Apply transform: skew(20deg, 10deg); to .skew-box to skew it on the X and Y axes.

3. **Expected Output**: The skewed box should appear tilted along both axes.

Exercise 5: Combining Transformations

1. **Objective**: Apply multiple transformations to an element.

2. **Steps**:

   - In styles.css, combine transformations in .box:

```
.box {
  transform: translate(50px, 20px) scale(1.1) rotate(30deg);
}
```

3. **Expected Output:** The box should appear shifted, slightly enlarged, and rotated.

Lesson 26: Responsive Images and the <picture> Element

Responsive images help ensure that your website loads quickly and looks great on different screen sizes and resolutions. HTML provides several methods to handle responsive images, including the <picture> element and the srcset attribute.

1. srcset and sizes Attributes

The srcset attribute allows you to specify different image sources for different screen resolutions. The sizes attribute tells the browser how large the image will be on the page.

Example:

<img src="image-small.jpg"

   srcset="image-small.jpg 400w, image-medium.jpg 800w, image-large.jpg 1200w"

   sizes="(max-width: 600px) 100vw, 50vw"

   alt="A sample responsive image">

- **srcset**: Specifies multiple image files with their widths (e.g., 400w for 400 pixels wide).
- **sizes**: Specifies how much space the image takes up on the screen (e.g., 100vw for 100% of the viewport width).

2. The <picture> Element

The <picture> element provides more control, allowing you to specify multiple image formats and sources based on device or screen size. It's useful for art direction, where you might want different images for mobile and desktop views.

Example:

```
<picture>

  <source media="(max-width: 600px)" srcset="image-small.jpg">

  <source media="(min-width: 601px)" srcset="image-large.jpg">

  <img src="image-default.jpg" alt="A responsive image using the picture
element">

</picture>
```

In this example:

- **<source>**: Specifies the image source for certain conditions (e.g., (max-width: 600px) for screens 600px or narrower).

- **<img>**: Acts as a fallback if no conditions are met or if the browser doesn't support the <picture> element.

3. Responsive Images with Art Direction

The <picture> element also lets you provide different images for different screen orientations or formats.

Example:

```
<picture>

  <source media="(orientation: portrait)" srcset="image-portrait.jpg">

  <source media="(orientation: landscape)" srcset="image-
landscape.jpg">

  <img src="image-default.jpg" alt="Responsive image based on
orientation">

</picture>
```

4. Using WebP Format for Optimized Images

WebP is a modern image format that provides superior compression, helping reduce load times without sacrificing quality. The <picture> element makes it easy to provide WebP images with a fallback for browsers that don't support it.

Example:

```
<picture>

  <source type="image/webp" srcset="image.webp">

  <source type="image/jpeg" srcset="image.jpg">

  <img src="image.jpg" alt="Optimized image with WebP fallback">

</picture>
```

Practice Task

1. Add the following code to index.html to test responsive images with srcset and the <picture> element.

Example HTML (index.html):

```
<h2>Responsive Image with srcset</h2>

<img src="image-small.jpg"

  srcset="image-small.jpg 400w, image-medium.jpg 800w, image-large.jpg 1200w"

  sizes="(max-width: 600px) 100vw, (max-width: 1200px) 50vw, 33vw"

  alt="A responsive image using srcset">


<h2>Responsive Image with the Picture Element</h2>

<picture>

  <source media="(max-width: 600px)" srcset="image-small.jpg">
```

```
  <source media="(min-width: 601px)" srcset="image-large.jpg">

  <img src="image-default.jpg" alt="Responsive image using the picture
element">

</picture>
```

Responsive Image with WebP and JPEG Fallback

```
<picture>

  <source type="image/webp" srcset="image.webp">

  <source type="image/jpeg" srcset="image.jpg">

  <img src="image.jpg" alt="Optimized image with WebP fallback">

</picture>
```

2. Save the file and open index.html in your browser. Resize the browser window to test how the images adapt based on screen size and device orientation.

Experiment with different image resolutions and formats for testing purposes.

Lesson 26 Exercises: Practicing Responsive Images and the <picture> Element

In this lesson, you'll learn to use the srcset attribute and the <picture> element to ensure images adapt to different screen sizes and resolutions.

Exercise 1: Using srcset for Responsive Images

1. **Objective**: Serve different image sizes based on screen resolution.

2. **Steps**:

    o   In index.html, add an image tag:

```
<img src="small-image.jpg"

  srcset="small-image.jpg 400w, medium-image.jpg 800w, large-image.jpg 1200w"

  sizes="(max-width: 600px) 100vw, 50vw"

  alt="A sample responsive image">
```

    o   Ensure you have images with different sizes saved (e.g., small-image.jpg, medium-image.jpg, large-image.jpg).

3. **Expected Output**: The browser should load different images based on screen width, using the smallest version on narrow screens and larger versions on wide screens.

Exercise 2: Using the <picture> Element for Art Direction

1. **Objective**: Display different images based on screen size for art direction.

2. **Steps**:

    o   In index.html, add a <picture> element:

```
<picture>
```

```
<source media="(max-width: 600px)" srcset="image-small.jpg">

<source media="(min-width: 601px)" srcset="image-large.jpg">

<img src="image-default.jpg" alt="Responsive image based on screen size">

</picture>
```

- o Use image-small.jpg for screens 600px or smaller, image-large.jpg for larger screens, and provide a default image-default.jpg for fallback.

3. **Expected Output**: The image should change based on screen width, displaying a different version for mobile and desktop.

Exercise 3: Adding WebP Format with Fallback

1. **Objective**: Use WebP format for optimized image loading with a JPEG fallback.

2. **Steps**:

- o In index.html, modify the <picture> element to add WebP format support:

```
<picture>

  <source type="image/webp" srcset="image.webp">

  <source type="image/jpeg" srcset="image.jpg">

  <img src="image.jpg" alt="Optimized image with WebP fallback">

</picture>
```

- o Ensure you have both image.webp and image.jpg saved in your project folder.

3. **Expected Output**: Modern browsers should load the WebP format, while older browsers fall back to the JPEG version.

Exercise 4: Using srcset and sizes for Retina Displays

1. **Objective**: Serve high-resolution images on retina displays.

2. **Steps**:

   o In index.html, add an image with srcset that targets retina displays:

```
<img src="image-1x.jpg"
  srcset="image-1x.jpg 1x, image-2x.jpg 2x"
  alt="High-resolution image for retina display">
```

   o Use image-1x.jpg for standard screens and image-2x.jpg for retina screens.

3. **Expected Output**: The browser should load the high-resolution image on retina displays and the standard image on regular displays.

Lesson 27: Introduction to CSS Frameworks (Bootstrap)

CSS frameworks like **Bootstrap** provide pre-designed components and styles, helping you quickly build responsive and visually appealing web pages. Bootstrap, one of the most popular frameworks, includes a responsive grid system, buttons, forms, navigation bars, and more.

1. Setting Up Bootstrap

To use Bootstrap, include its CSS and JavaScript files in your HTML. You can add it via a CDN (Content Delivery Network).

Add Bootstrap to Your HTML:

```
<head>

  <link rel="stylesheet" href="https://cdnjs.cloudflare.com/ajax/libs/bootstrap/5.1.3/css/bootstrap.min.css">

  <script src="https://cdnjs.cloudflare.com/ajax/libs/bootstrap/5.1.3/js/bootstrap.bundle.min.js"></script>

</head>
```

2. Bootstrap Grid System

Bootstrap's grid system helps create responsive layouts using rows and columns. It's based on a 12-column layout, where you can specify the number of columns an element should span based on screen size.

- **Basic Grid Structure:**
    - Use .container for a responsive container.
    - Use .row to create rows.

  o Use .col or .col-* (e.g., .col-6 for half-width) to create columns.

Example:

```
<div class="container">

  <div class="row">

    <div class="col-md-6">Column 1 (50% width on medium screens)</div>

    <div class="col-md-6">Column 2 (50% width on medium screens)</div>

  </div>

</div>
```

3. Responsive Classes

Bootstrap uses responsive class prefixes to adjust column widths on different screen sizes:

- **col-xs-*** (extra small, for mobile)

- **col-sm-*** (small, for tablets)

- **col-md-*** (medium, for desktops)

- **col-lg-*** (large, for larger desktops)

Example:

```
<div class="row">

  <div class="col-12 col-md-6">Column 1</div> <!-- Full-width on mobile, half-width on desktop -->

  <div class="col-12 col-md-6">Column 2</div>

</div>
```

4. Bootstrap Components

Bootstrap includes many pre-styled components, like buttons, forms, navigation bars, and cards.

- **Buttons:**

```
<button class="btn btn-primary">Primary Button</button>
```

```
<button class="btn btn-secondary">Secondary Button</button>
```

- **Form Controls:**

```
<form>
  <div class="mb-3">
    <label for="exampleInputEmail1" class="form-label">Email address</label>
    <input type="email" class="form-control" id="exampleInputEmail1" aria-describedby="emailHelp">
  </div>
  <button type="submit" class="btn btn-primary">Submit</button>
</form>
```

- **Navigation Bar:**

```
<nav class="navbar navbar-expand-lg navbar-light bg-light">
  <a class="navbar-brand" href="#">Navbar</a>
  <button class="navbar-toggler" type="button" data-bs-toggle="collapse" data-bs-target="#navbarNav">
    <span class="navbar-toggler-icon"></span>
  </button>
  <div class="collapse navbar-collapse" id="navbarNav">
    <ul class="navbar-nav">
      <li class="nav-item"><a class="nav-link active" href="#">Home</a></li>
```

```
        <li class="nav-item"><a class="nav-link" href="#">Features</a></li>

        <li class="nav-item"><a class="nav-link" href="#">Pricing</a></li>

      </ul>

    </div>

</nav>
```

- **Cards**:

```
<div class="card" style="width: 18rem;">

  <img src="card-image.jpg" class="card-img-top" alt="...">

  <div class="card-body">

    <h5 class="card-title">Card Title</h5>

    <p class="card-text">Some quick example text to build on the card
title.</p>

    <a href="#" class="btn btn-primary">Go somewhere</a>

  </div>

</div>
```

Practice Task

1. Add the following HTML code to index.html to test Bootstrap's grid and components.

Example HTML (index.html):

```
<!DOCTYPE html>

<html lang="en">

<head>

  <meta charset="UTF-8">
```

```html
  <meta name="viewport" content="width=device-width, initial-scale=1.0">

  <title>Bootstrap Example</title>

  <link rel="stylesheet" href="https://cdnjs.cloudflare.com/ajax/libs/bootstrap/5.1.3/css/bootstrap.min.css">

  <script src="https://cdnjs.cloudflare.com/ajax/libs/bootstrap/5.1.3/js/bootstrap.bundle.min.js"></script>

</head>

<body>


<!-- Navbar -->

<nav class="navbar navbar-expand-lg navbar-light bg-light">

  <a class="navbar-brand" href="#">Navbar</a>

  <button class="navbar-toggler" type="button" data-bs-toggle="collapse" data-bs-target="#navbarNav">

    <span class="navbar-toggler-icon"></span>

  </button>

  <div class="collapse navbar-collapse" id="navbarNav">

    <ul class="navbar-nav">

      <li class="nav-item"><a class="nav-link active" href="#">Home</a></li>

      <li class="nav-item"><a class="nav-link" href="#">Features</a></li>

      <li class="nav-item"><a class="nav-link" href="#">Pricing</a></li>

    </ul>

  </div>

</nav>
```

```html
<!-- Grid System -->
<div class="container mt-5">
  <div class="row">
    <div class="col-md-6">Column 1</div>
    <div class="col-md-6">Column 2</div>
  </div>
</div>


<!-- Buttons -->
<div class="container mt-3">
  <button class="btn btn-primary">Primary Button</button>
  <button class="btn btn-secondary">Secondary Button</button>
</div>


<!-- Card -->
<div class="container mt-3">
  <div class="card" style="width: 18rem;">
    <img src="card-image.jpg" class="card-img-top" alt="...">
    <div class="card-body">
      <h5 class="card-title">Card Title</h5>
      <p class="card-text">Some quick example text to build on the card
title.</p>
      <a href="#" class="btn btn-primary">Go somewhere</a>
    </div>
```

```
    </div>

</div>


</body>

</html>
```

2. Open index.html in your browser to see the Bootstrap components in action.

Try experimenting with other Bootstrap components, like modals, alerts, or carousels.

Lesson 27 Exercises: Practicing Bootstrap for Responsive Design

In this lesson, you'll use Bootstrap's grid system and components to build a responsive layout quickly.

Exercise 1: Setting Up a Basic Bootstrap Grid

1. **Objective**: Use Bootstrap's grid system to create a responsive layout.

2. **Steps**:

   o   Add the Bootstrap CDN link to your index.html <head>:

```
<link rel="stylesheet"
href="https://cdnjs.cloudflare.com/ajax/libs/bootstrap/5.1.3/css/bootstrap.
min.css">
```

   o   In the body, create a <div class="container"> and add a .row inside it with three .col-md-4 columns.

   o   Inside each column, add a <p> with sample text.

3. **Expected Output**: On medium and larger screens, the text should display in three columns, while on smaller screens, each column should stack vertically.

Exercise 2: Using Bootstrap Buttons

1. **Objective**: Add styled buttons using Bootstrap.

2. **Steps**:

   o   In index.html, add a few buttons with different Bootstrap classes:

```
<button class="btn btn-primary">Primary Button</button>

<button class="btn btn-secondary">Secondary Button</button>
```

```
<button class="btn btn-success">Success Button</button>
```

3. **Expected Output:** Each button should display with the specific Bootstrap styles, each with a different color.

Exercise 3: Creating a Responsive Navigation Bar

1. **Objective:** Use Bootstrap's navigation bar component.

2. **Steps:**

   o In index.html, add the following Bootstrap navbar at the top of the body:

```
<nav class="navbar navbar-expand-lg navbar-light bg-light">

  <a class="navbar-brand" href="#">My Site</a>

  <button class="navbar-toggler" type="button" data-bs-toggle="collapse"
data-bs-target="#navbarNav">

    <span class="navbar-toggler-icon"></span>

  </button>

  <div class="collapse navbar-collapse" id="navbarNav">

    <ul class="navbar-nav">

      <li class="nav-item"><a class="nav-link active"
href="#">Home</a></li>

      <li class="nav-item"><a class="nav-link" href="#">About</a></li>

      <li class="nav-item"><a class="nav-link" href="#">Contact</a></li>

    </ul>

  </div>

</nav>
```

   o Include the Bootstrap JavaScript bundle in the <body> or at the end of your page for the navbar to work:

```
<script
src="https://cdnjs.cloudflare.com/ajax/libs/bootstrap/5.1.3/js/bootstrap.bu
ndle.min.js"></script>
```

3. **Expected Output**: You should see a responsive navigation bar that collapses into a hamburger menu on smaller screens.

Exercise 4: Using Bootstrap Cards for Content Sections

1. **Objective**: Display content in a card format using Bootstrap.

2. **Steps**:

   o In index.html, create a .container with three Bootstrap .card components, each inside a .col-md-4.

   o Use the following template for each card:

```
<div class="card" style="width: 18rem;">

  <img src="card-image.jpg" class="card-img-top" alt="...">

  <div class="card-body">

    <h5 class="card-title">Card Title</h5>

    <p class="card-text">Some example text to build on the card title.</p>

    <a href="#" class="btn btn-primary">Learn More</a>

  </div>

</div>
```

3. **Expected Output**: Each card should display an image, title, text, and button, and the layout should adjust to fit the screen size.

Lesson 28: Introduction to SCSS (Sass)

Sass (Syntactically Awesome Style Sheets) is a CSS preprocessor that adds powerful features to CSS, like variables, nesting, mixins, and functions. **SCSS** (Sassy CSS) is one of the two syntax options of Sass, using the same syntax as CSS but with added functionalities.

1. Setting Up SCSS

To use SCSS, you need a compiler to convert SCSS files into regular CSS that browsers understand. Popular options include **Dart Sass** (command line), **Live Sass Compiler** (VS Code extension), or build tools like **Webpack**.

2. Variables

SCSS variables allow you to store values like colors, fonts, and sizes for reuse across your styles.

Example:

```scss
// Variables

$primary-color: #3498db;

$secondary-color: #2980b9;

$font-size-large: 24px;


body {

  background-color: $primary-color;

  color: #333;

}


h1 {

  color: $secondary-color;
```

```scss
  font-size: $font-size-large;

}
```

3. Nesting

SCSS allows you to nest selectors, making your code more organized, especially for deeply nested HTML structures.

Example:

```scss
// Nested selectors

nav {

  background-color: $primary-color;


  ul {

    list-style: none;


    li {

      display: inline-block;

      padding: 10px;


      a {

        color: white;

        text-decoration: none;

      }
    }
  }
}
```

4. Mixins

Mixins let you define reusable chunks of code, useful for applying the same set of properties across different elements.

Example:

```scss
// Mixin for button styling

@mixin button-style($bg-color, $text-color) {

    background-color: $bg-color;

    color: $text-color;

    padding: 10px 20px;

    border-radius: 5px;

    cursor: pointer;

    text-align: center;


    &:hover {

      background-color: darken($bg-color, 10%);

    }

}


button.primary {

    @include button-style($primary-color, white);

}


button.secondary {

    @include button-style($secondary-color, white);
```

```
}
```

5. Inheritance

SCSS allows elements to inherit properties from other selectors using the @extend directive, helping reduce redundancy.

Example:

```scss
// Base button style

%button-base {

    padding: 10px 20px;

    border-radius: 5px;

    cursor: pointer;

}


button.primary {

    @extend %button-base;

    background-color: $primary-color;

    color: white;

}
```

6. Partials and Imports

You can organize SCSS code into multiple files, called **partials**. Partial filenames start with an underscore (e.g., _variables.scss). Import them into a main file using @import.

Example:

```scss
// In _variables.scss

$primary-color: #3498db;
```

```
// In _buttons.scss

@import 'variables';


button.primary {

  background-color: $primary-color;

}


// In main.scss

@import 'variables';

@import 'buttons';
```

Practice Task

1. If using VS Code, install the **Live Sass Compiler** extension, which compiles SCSS files to CSS in real-time.

2. Create an SCSS file (e.g., styles.scss) and add the following SCSS code.

Example SCSS File (styles.scss):

```
// Variables

$primary-color: #3498db;

$secondary-color: #2980b9;

$font-size-large: 24px;


// Mixin

@mixin button-style($bg-color, $text-color) {
```

```scss
    background-color: $bg-color;

    color: $text-color;

    padding: 10px 20px;

    border-radius: 5px;

    cursor: pointer;

    text-align: center;


    &:hover {

      background-color: darken($bg-color, 10%);

    }

  }


  // Styling

  body {

    font-family: Arial, sans-serif;

    background-color: $primary-color;

    color: white;

  }


  h1 {

    font-size: $font-size-large;

    color: $secondary-color;

  }


  button.primary {
```

```
    @include button-style($primary-color, white);

}


button.secondary {

    @include button-style($secondary-color, white);

}
```

3. Compile styles.scss to CSS and link the generated CSS file in index.html.

Example HTML (index.html):

```html
<!DOCTYPE html>

<html lang="en">

<head>

    <meta charset="UTF-8">

    <meta name="viewport" content="width=device-width, initial-scale=1.0">

    <title>SCSS Example</title>

    <link rel="stylesheet" href="styles.css"> <!-- Link compiled CSS file -->

</head>

<body>


<h1>Welcome to SCSS Styling</h1>

<button class="primary">Primary Button</button>

<button class="secondary">Secondary Button</button>
```

```
</body>

</html>
```

4. Open index.html in your browser to see the styled elements.

Experiment with other SCSS features like functions and loops.

Lesson 28 Exercises: Practicing SCSS Features

In this lesson, you'll work with SCSS features like variables, nesting, and mixins to make your CSS code more efficient and organized.

Exercise 1: Using Variables in SCSS

1. **Objective**: Define and use SCSS variables for colors and fonts.

2. **Steps**:

   o In styles.scss, add the following variables:

$primary-color: #3498db;

$secondary-color: #2980b9;

$font-family: Arial, sans-serif;

   o Use $primary-color for the background color of your <body>, $secondary-color for the color of <h2> elements, and $font-family as the default font for the entire page.

3. **Expected Output**: Your page should display the colors and fonts based on the defined SCSS variables.

Exercise 2: Nesting Selectors

1. **Objective**: Use nested selectors for a structured layout.

2. **Steps**:

   o In index.html, create a navigation menu with a <nav> containing a <ul> with several <li><a> items.

   o In styles.scss, add the following nested structure:

```
nav {
  background-color: $primary-color;
```

```scss
ul {
  list-style: none;
  padding: 0;
  li {
    display: inline-block;
    margin-right: 10px;
    a {
      color: white;
      text-decoration: none;
      &:hover {
        color: $secondary-color;
      }
    }
  }
}
```

3. **Expected Output**: The nested SCSS selectors should apply styles to the navigation menu, with a hover effect that changes link color.

Exercise 3: Creating and Using Mixins

1. **Objective**: Create a mixin to reuse button styles.

2. **Steps**:

   o In styles.scss, create a mixin named button-style that takes two arguments for background and text color:

```scss
@mixin button-style($bg-color, $text-color) {
  background-color: $bg-color;
```

```scss
    color: $text-color;

    padding: 10px 20px;

    border-radius: 5px;

    cursor: pointer;

    &:hover {

      background-color: darken($bg-color, 10%);

    }

}
```

- o Apply the mixin to two different buttons in your HTML, using @include button-style($primary-color, white); and @include button-style($secondary-color, white);.

3. **Expected Output**: Both buttons should have a consistent style, with hover effects that darken the background color.

Exercise 4: Using Partials and Imports

1. **Objective**: Organize SCSS code into multiple files.

2. **Steps**:

   - o Create three SCSS partial files: _variables.scss, _buttons.scss, and _layout.scss.

   - o Move your variables to _variables.scss, your button mixin to _buttons.scss, and any layout styling to _layout.scss.

   - o In styles.scss, import the partials:

```scss
@import 'variables';

@import 'buttons';

@import 'layout';
```

3. **Expected Output**: Your SCSS code should be more organized, with styles split into different files and imported into the main styles.scss.

Lesson 29: HTML and CSS Accessibility Best Practices

Making your website accessible ensures that people with disabilities can use and navigate it. Accessible websites are easier to use for everyone and comply with legal standards in many regions.

1. Using Semantic HTML

Semantic HTML elements provide meaning and structure to your content, helping screen readers understand the layout. For example:

- Use <header>, <nav>, <main>, <section>, and <footer> to define the page structure.

- Use <button> for interactive elements instead of <div> or <span>, as it's inherently accessible.

Example:

```
<header>
  <h1>Website Title</h1>
</header>
<main>
  <section>
    <h2>About Us</h2>
    <p>Information about our website.</p>
  </section>
</main>
```

2. Providing Text Alternatives for Images

Images should include alt attributes describing the image. If an image is purely decorative, use an empty alt="" to inform screen readers to ignore it.

Example:

```
<img src="logo.png" alt="Company Logo">
```

```
<img src="decorative.png" alt="">
```

3. Using Descriptive Link Text

Link text should describe the destination. Avoid generic text like "click here" or "read more."

Example:

```
<a href="services.html">Learn more about our services</a>
```

4. Ensuring Keyboard Accessibility

All interactive elements (e.g., links, buttons, and forms) should be accessible via keyboard. Avoid tabindex values outside the default flow, and use tabindex="0" on non-focusable elements if necessary.

Example:

```
<div tabindex="0">This is a keyboard-accessible div</div>
```

5. Adding ARIA (Accessible Rich Internet Applications) Attributes

ARIA attributes add accessibility for custom or dynamic elements. However, ARIA should complement, not replace, semantic HTML.

- **aria-label**: Provides a label for an element.
- **aria-labelledby**: Links an element to a label.

- **aria-live**: Defines regions for screen reader announcements (useful for dynamic content).

Example:

```
<button aria-label="Close the modal">×</button>
```

```
<div aria-live="polite">Content updated</div>
```

6. Using Sufficient Color Contrast

Ensure text contrasts enough with its background for readability. Aim for a **contrast ratio** of at least **4.5:1** for normal text and **3:1** for large text.

Example:

```css
/* High contrast */
body {
    background-color: #ffffff;
    color: #333333;
}
```

7. Styling Focus States

Use :focus styles to visually indicate when an element is selected with the keyboard, helping users navigate with the Tab key.

Example:

```css
button:focus {
    outline: 3px solid #3498db;
}
```

8. Using Forms with Accessible Labels

Ensure form elements have descriptive labels. Use <label> elements and associate them with inputs via the for attribute.

Example:

<label for="email">Email:</label>

<input type="email" id="email" name="email" required>

Practice Task

1. Add the following HTML and CSS code to index.html and styles.css to practice accessibility.

Example HTML (index.html):

<!DOCTYPE html>

<html lang="en">

<head>

  <meta charset="UTF-8">

  <meta name="viewport" content="width=device-width, initial-scale=1.0">

  <title>Accessible Website Example</title>

  <link rel="stylesheet" href="styles.css">

</head>

<body>

<header>

  <h1>Accessible Website</h1>

</header>

```
<main>

  <section aria-labelledby="about-heading">

    <h2 id="about-heading">About Our Website</h2>

    <p>Our mission is to create accessible web experiences for
everyone.</p>

    <a href="services.html">Learn more about our services</a>

  </section>


  <form>

    <label for="username">Username</label>

    <input type="text" id="username" name="username" aria-
required="true" required>


    <label for="email">Email</label>

    <input type="email" id="email" name="email" required>


    <button type="submit">Submit</button>

  </form>

</main>


</body>

</html>
```

Example CSS (styles.css):

```
/* High Contrast Text */
```

```css
body {

  background-color: #ffffff;

  color: #333333;

  font-family: Arial, sans-serif;

}


/* Focus State */

button:focus,

input:focus {

  outline: 3px solid #3498db;

}


/* Link Styling */

a {

  color: #3498db;

}


a:focus,

a:hover {

  color: #2980b9;

}
```

2. Save both files and open index.html in your browser to review the accessible elements and keyboard navigation.

Experiment with different ARIA roles and additional contrast colors.

Lesson 29 Exercises: HTML and CSS Accessibility Best Practices

In Lesson 29, you'll apply accessibility best practices to ensure your webpage is inclusive and user-friendly. You'll focus on using semantic HTML, adding text alternatives for images, improving link clarity, and making interactive elements keyboard-accessible.

Exercise 1: Using Semantic HTML

1. **Objective**: Improve the HTML structure by using semantic tags.

2. **Steps**:

   o Replace any non-semantic <div> and <span> elements that are used solely for layout with appropriate semantic tags (<header>, <nav>, <main>, <section>, <footer>, etc.).

   o Ensure each section has a heading tag (<h1>, <h2>, etc.) to improve the content structure for screen readers.

3. **Expected Outcome**: Your HTML should be organized with semantic elements, enhancing clarity and navigation for screen readers and search engines.

Exercise 2: Providing Text Alternatives for Images

1. **Objective**: Ensure all images have meaningful alt attributes.

2. **Steps**:

   o Review all <img> elements in your HTML.

   o Add an alt attribute to each image, describing its content and purpose (e.g., "Profile picture of John Doe").

   o If an image is decorative and does not convey essential information, set alt="" to signal screen readers to skip it.

3. **Expected Outcome**: Every image should now have an appropriate alt attribute, ensuring visually impaired users understand the content or function of each image.

Exercise 3: Using Descriptive Link Text

1. **Objective**: Make link text descriptive and contextually meaningful.

2. **Steps**:

   o Review all <a> elements in your HTML.

   o Replace vague link text like "click here" with descriptive phrases (e.g., change "click here to learn more" to "Learn more about our services").

3. **Expected Outcome**: All links should have clear, descriptive text that provides context for where the link leads, enhancing navigation for screen reader users.

Exercise 4: Keyboard Accessibility Check

1. **Objective**: Ensure all interactive elements are accessible via keyboard navigation.

2. **Steps**:

   o Use the Tab key to navigate through your webpage.

   o Verify that all interactive elements (links, buttons, and form fields) are accessible and visually indicated when focused.

   o If any elements are missing focus styles, add them in your CSS with :focus pseudo-class (e.g., button:focus { outline: 2px solid #3498db; }).

3. **Expected Outcome**: Every interactive element on your page should be accessible with the keyboard and visibly highlighted when focused, providing a better experience for users who rely on keyboard navigation.

Exercise 5: Adding ARIA Attributes for Accessibility

1. **Objective**: Improve accessibility by adding ARIA attributes where needed.

2. **Steps**:

   o   Identify interactive elements or custom components that might need additional context for screen readers.

   o   Add ARIA attributes like aria-label, aria-labelledby, or aria-hidden where appropriate. For example, if you have an icon-only button, add aria-label="Open menu" to describe its action.

3. **Expected Outcome**: Your page should include ARIA attributes on relevant elements, improving the user experience for screen reader users.

Lesson 30: Building a Complete Web Page Project

In this lesson, we'll combine HTML, CSS, and some of the advanced features you've learned to create a simple, accessible, and responsive web page. The project will include a header, navigation, hero section, services section, and a contact form.

Project Structure

Sections of the Page:

1. **Header and Navigation**: Fixed at the top with a responsive menu.
2. **Hero Section**: A welcome message with a background image.
3. **Services Section**: Describes three services.
4. **Contact Form**: A simple form with basic validation.

Step 1: HTML Structure

Create the HTML structure, including semantic elements like <header>, <main>, and <footer>.

Example HTML (index.html):

```
<!DOCTYPE html>

<html lang="en">

<head>

  <meta charset="UTF-8">

  <meta name="viewport" content="width=device-width, initial-scale=1.0">
```

```html
    <title>My Portfolio</title>
    <link rel="stylesheet" href="styles.css">
</head>
<body>

<header>
  <nav class="navbar">
    <a href="#" class="logo">My Portfolio</a>
    <ul class="nav-links">
      <li><a href="#hero">Home</a></li>
      <li><a href="#services">Services</a></li>
      <li><a href="#contact">Contact</a></li>
    </ul>
  </nav>
</header>

<main>
  <!-- Hero Section -->
  <section id="hero" class="hero">
    <h1>Welcome to My Portfolio</h1>
    <p>Creating accessible and responsive websites.</p>
  </section>

  <!-- Services Section -->
  <section id="services" class="services">
```

```html
<h2>Our Services</h2>
<div class="service-item">
  <h3>Web Design</h3>
  <p>Beautiful, responsive designs tailored to your needs.</p>
</div>
<div class="service-item">
  <h3>Development</h3>
  <p>Efficient and accessible code for optimal performance.</p>
</div>
<div class="service-item">
  <h3>SEO</h3>
  <p>Improving visibility and search engine rankings.</p>
</div>
</section>


<!-- Contact Form -->
<section id="contact" class="contact">
  <h2>Contact Us</h2>
  <form>
    <label for="name">Name</label>
    <input type="text" id="name" name="name" required>

    <label for="email">Email</label>
    <input type="email" id="email" name="email" required>
```

```
    <label for="message">Message</label>

    <textarea id="message" name="message" rows="4"
required></textarea>


    <button type="submit">Send Message</button>
  </form>
  </section>
</main>


<footer>
  <p>&copy; 2023 My Portfolio. All rights reserved.</p>
</footer>


</body>
</html>
```

Step 2: CSS Styling

Add styles for layout, typography, colors, and responsiveness.

Example CSS (styles.css):

```css
/* General Styles */
body {
  font-family: Arial, sans-serif;
  margin: 0;
  padding: 0;
```

```css
    line-height: 1.6;

}


header {

    background-color: #333;

    padding: 10px;

    color: #fff;

    position: fixed;

    width: 100%;

    top: 0;

    z-index: 10;

}


.navbar {

    display: flex;

    justify-content: space-between;

    align-items: center;

}


.nav-links {

    list-style: none;

    display: flex;

    gap: 15px;

}
```

```css
.nav-links a {
  color: white;
  text-decoration: none;
}

.hero {
  display: flex;
  flex-direction: column;
  align-items: center;
  justify-content: center;
  height: 100vh;
  background: url('hero-background.jpg') no-repeat center center/cover;
  color: white;
  text-align: center;
}

.services {
  padding: 50px 20px;
  background-color: #f0f0f0;
  text-align: center;
}

.service-item {
  margin: 20px;
  padding: 20px;
```

```css
  background-color: white;

  box-shadow: 0 4px 8px rgba(0,0,0,0.1);

  border-radius: 5px;

}


.contact {

  padding: 50px 20px;

  background-color: #e0e0e0;

  text-align: center;

}


.contact form {

  max-width: 600px;

  margin: auto;

  text-align: left;

}


.contact label {

  display: block;

  margin-top: 10px;

}


.contact input,
.contact textarea {

  width: 100%;
```

```css
  padding: 10px;

  margin-top: 5px;

  border-radius: 4px;

  border: 1px solid #ccc;

}


button {

  padding: 10px 20px;

  background-color: #3498db;

  color: white;

  border: none;

  border-radius: 5px;

  cursor: pointer;

  margin-top: 10px;

}


button:hover {

  background-color: #2980b9;

}


footer {

  padding: 20px;

  background-color: #333;

  color: white;

  text-align: center;
```

```css
}


/* Responsive Styles */

@media (max-width: 768px) {

  .nav-links {

    flex-direction: column;

    gap: 10px;

  }


  .service-item {

    margin: 10px 0;

  }

}
```

Step 3: Final Touches

1. Add a hero-background.jpg image to your project folder or update the background property in .hero to use an image URL of your choice.

2. Save both files and open index.html in your browser to view your completed project.

Feel free to customize the colors, fonts, or images to make it your own. You now have a foundational structure for building more advanced web pages!

Lesson 30 Exercises: Building a Complete Web Page Project

In Lesson 30, you'll bring everything together by creating a complete, accessible, and responsive webpage that showcases your HTML, CSS, and accessibility skills. This project will reinforce everything you've learned in this course.

Exercise 1: Building the Basic HTML Structure

1. **Objective**: Set up a well-structured HTML document.

2. **Steps**:

   - Create a new file named index.html.

   - Add a <header> containing a <nav> with links to different sections (e.g., Home, Services, Contact).

   - In <main>, create sections like "Hero," "Services," and "Contact."

   - Add a <footer> with basic copyright information.

   - Use semantic HTML elements and make sure each section has an appropriate heading (<h1>, <h2>, etc.).

3. **Expected Outcome**: A clean HTML structure that includes a header, main content, and footer with semantic tags.

Exercise 2: Styling with CSS

1. **Objective**: Apply CSS to style the layout and enhance visual appeal.

2. **Steps**:

   - Create styles.css and link it to your HTML file.

   - Style each section with CSS properties such as background-color, padding, and margin.

       o   Use the CSS Flexbox or Grid layout to organize content within sections (e.g., use Flexbox for the navigation links).

3. **Expected Outcome**: Your webpage should have a visually cohesive style, with well-organized content and spacing.

Exercise 3: Making the Design Responsive

1. **Objective**: Ensure your layout adapts to different screen sizes.

2. **Steps**:

       o   Use CSS media queries in styles.css to create responsive layouts:

           ▪   Stack navigation links vertically on smaller screens.

           ▪   Adjust font sizes and section spacing for mobile.

       o   Test your webpage by resizing the browser window and checking it on a mobile device if possible.

3. **Expected Outcome**: Your webpage should adjust to fit both desktop and mobile screen sizes, providing a good user experience on all devices.

Exercise 4: Adding Interactive and Visual Effects

1. **Objective**: Enhance the user experience with transitions and a theme toggle.

2. **Steps**:

       o   Add a hover effect to links and buttons using CSS transitions.

       o   Implement a JavaScript function to toggle between light and dark themes:

```
function toggleTheme() {

   document.body.classList.toggle('dark-theme');
```

```
}
```

- o Style the dark-theme class in styles.css by switching background and text colors:

```
.dark-theme {
  background-color: #333;
  color: #fff;
}
```

3. **Expected Outcome**: The theme should toggle between light and dark when activated, and links/buttons should have smooth hover effects.

Exercise 5: Performing an Accessibility Audit

1. **Objective**: Check for and improve accessibility.

2. **Steps**:

- o Review your HTML and ensure all images have meaningful alt attributes, and links have descriptive text.

- o Test your page's keyboard accessibility by navigating through each element with the Tab key.

- o Run your page through an accessibility checker (e.g., WAVE Web Accessibility Tool) and make any recommended improvements.

3. **Expected Outcome**: Your webpage should be accessible, providing a smooth experience for all users.

Bonus Exercise: Adding a Portfolio Section

1. **Objective**: Add an additional portfolio or gallery section to showcase your work.

2. **Steps**:

- o In the main content area, add a "Portfolio" section with images or project cards.

- o Style the portfolio section using CSS Grid for a gallery layout, with each item linking to more details.

3. **Expected Outcome**: The portfolio section should display as a visually pleasing gallery and link to more project details or larger images.

By completing these exercises, you will create a professional, fully responsive, and accessible webpage that demonstrates your HTML, CSS, and accessibility skills!

Congratulations on completing the course!